Romans

Romans

DAILY SEEDS

Romans

FROM SIN MANAGEMENT TO LOVE UNLEASHED

J. D. Walt

ZONDERVAN REFLECTIVE

Romans
Copyright © 2025 by J. D. Walt

Published by Zondervan, 3950 Sparks Drive SE, Suite 101, Grand Rapids, MI 49546, USA. Zondervan is a registered trademark of The Zondervan Corporation, L.L.C., a wholly owned subsidiary of HarperCollins Christian Publishing, Inc.

Requests for information should be addressed to customercare@harpercollins.com.

Zondervan titles may be purchased in bulk for educational, business, fundraising, or sales promotional use. For information, please email SpecialMarkets@Zondervan.com.

ISBN 978-0-310-17170-6 (softcover)
ISBN 978-0-310-17172-0 (audio)
ISBN 978-0-310-17171-3 (ebook)

Unless otherwise noted, Scripture quotations are taken from The Holy Bible, New International Version®, NIV®. Copyright © 1973, 1978, 1984, 2011 by Biblica, Inc.® Used by permission of Zondervan. All rights reserved worldwide. www.Zondervan.com. The "NIV" and "New International Version" are trademarks registered in the United States Patent and Trademark Office by Biblica, Inc.®

Scripture quotations marked ESV are taken from the ESV® Bible (The Holy Bible, English Standard Version®). Copyright © 2001 by Crossway, a publishing ministry of Good News Publishers. Used by permission. All rights reserved.

Scripture quotations marked KJV are taken from the King James Version. Public domain.

Scripture quotations marked NASB are taken from the (NASB®) New American Standard Bible®. Copyright © 1960, 1971, 1977, 1995, 2020 by The Lockman Foundation. Used by permission. All rights reserved. www.lockman.org.

Scripture quotations marked NRSVue are taken from the New Revised Standard Version Updated Edition. Copyright © 2021 National Council of Churches of Christ in the United States of America. Used by permission. All rights reserved worldwide.

Scripture quotations marked OEB are taken from the Open English Bible, release 2022.1. Licensed under Creative Commons, CC0 1.0. https://openenglishbible.org.

Any internet addresses (websites, blogs, etc.) and telephone numbers in this book are offered as a resource. They are not intended in any way to be or imply an endorsement by Zondervan, nor does Zondervan vouch for the content of these sites and numbers for the life of this book.

All rights reserved. No part of this publication may be reproduced, stored in a retrieval system, or transmitted in any form or by any means—electronic, mechanical, photocopy, recording, or any other—except for brief quotations in printed reviews, without the prior permission of the publisher.

Without limiting the exclusive rights of any author, contributor or the publisher of this publication, any unauthorized use of this publication to train generative artificial intelligence (AI) technologies is expressly prohibited. HarperCollins also exercise their rights under Article 4(3) of the Digital Single Market Directive 2019/790 and expressly reserve this publication from the text and data mining exception.

HarperCollins Publishers, Macken House, 39/40 Mayor Street Upper, Dublin 1, D01 C9W8, Ireland (https://www.harpercollins.com)

Cover design and illustrations: Derek Thornton / Notch Design
Interior design: Denise Froehlich

$PrintCode

*For my children: David, Mary Kathryn, Lily,
and Samuel—our unbelievable, inconceivable,
unrepeatable miracles of God!*

Contents

Preface xi
How This Works xiii
Introduction xvii

Week 1: Romans 1:1–2:4

1. Romans 1:1–7: What Is Your Calling? 3
2. Romans 1:8–15: Give Me 100 5
3. Romans 1:16–17: How to Have a Blessed Life 8
4. Romans 1:18–23: From a Burning Bush to a Burning House 10
5. Romans 1:24–32: The Difference Between Our Sins and Our Sin .. 12
6. Romans 2:1–4: Reapproaching Repentance 14
7. Week 1: Discussion Questions 17

Week 2: Romans 2:5–3:18

8. Romans 2:5–11: Sin Swamp: Got to Go Through It. 21
9. Romans 2:12–16: On the Law, the Gospel, and the Religion of Weight Loss . 23
10. Romans 2:17–24: A Diatribe Against Self-Righteous Sinners ... 27
11. Romans 2:25–29: The Butterflied Heart 29
12. Romans 3:1–8: Before Jesus Lifts, Jesus Levels 33
13. Romans 3:9–18: Why There Is Only One Prayer 35
14. Week 2: Discussion Questions 38

Week 3: Romans 3:19–4:12

15. Romans 3:19–20: Jesus Paid It All 41
16. Romans 3:21–26: The Second Mic Drop in Romans 43
17. Romans 3:27–31: Has Anyone Ever Paid Your Debts? 45
18. Romans 4:1–3: Faith: From Beliefs to Believing 48
19. Romans 4:4–8: The Difference Between Knowing What We Believe and Knowing Who We Believe 50
20. Romans 4:9–12: The Man on the Middle Cross Said I Could Come . 53
21. Week 3: Discussion Questions 57

Week 4: Romans 4:13–5:17

22. Romans 4:13–17: Back to the Second Beginning 61
23. Romans 4:18–25: A Wretch like Me? 63
24. Romans 5:1–6: How Does Gravity Work? 66
25. Romans 5:7–8: The Word of the Day and of Eternity 69
26. Romans 5:9–11: How Much More? 71
27. Romans 5:12–17: There Are Only Two Stories 73
28. Week 4: Discussion Questions 76

Week 5: Romans 5:18–6:23

29. Romans 5:18–21: The Soundtrack of the Gospel 79
30. Romans 6:1–4: What Jesus Left Behind in the Tomb 83
31. Romans 6:5–10: The Day It Started Changing for Me 86
32. Romans 6:11–14: Why We Need a Better Bumper Sticker 88
33. Romans 6:15–18: The Problem of Vertigo 91
34. Romans 6:19–23: Moving from My Commitment to Jesus's Consecration .. 94
35. Week 5: Discussion Questions 98

Week 6: Romans 7:1–8:11

36. Romans 7:1–6: Facts Lead to Faith, and Faith Leads to Feelings
    (and Not the Other Way Around) 101
37. Romans 7:7–10: The Dastardly Broken Brokenness of the Human Race ... 104
38. Romans 7:11–13: Our Infinite Capacity for Self-Deception 107
39. Romans 7:14–20: Unos, Dos, Tres, Catorce . . . ? 110
40. Romans 7:21–25: The Reason We Stay Stuck in Vertigo
    and How to Get Free 113
41. Romans 8:1–11: Welcome to the Second Half of the Gospel 116
42. Week 6: Discussion Questions 119

Week 7: Romans 8:12–9:15

43. Romans 8:12–17: What I Do Every Morning and You Should Too 123
44. Romans 8:18–25: When I Feel like Ruins, You See Foundations 126
45. Romans 8:26–30: How the Spirit Turns Ruins into Foundations 128
46. Romans 8:31–39: Yes, David, This Is for Looking At 131
47. Romans 9:1–5: Finding Sorrow and Anguish Over My
    Lack of Sorrow and Anguish 134
48. Romans 9:6–15: A Practice Swing at Predestination 137
49. Week 7: Discussion Questions 141

Week 8: Romans 9:16–10:13

50. Romans 9:16–21: On the Backstory and the Cover Story 145
51. Romans 9:22–29: The First and Last Question of Any Theologian Worth Their Salt...148
52. Romans 9:30–33: Jesus and Paul Would Not Have Been Friends 151
53. Romans 10:1–4: On the Most Dangerous Condition in the World 154
54. Romans 10:5–9: The Simple, Succinct, Sophisticated, Comprehensive Gospel... 156
55. Romans 10:10–13: Everyone Who Calls on the Name of the Lord Will Be Saved.. 159
56. Week 8: Discussion Questions 162

Week 9: Romans 10:14–11:32

57. Romans 10:14–15: How Feet Become Beautiful...................... 165
58. Romans 10:16–21: How to Not Miss Jesus............................ 167
59. Romans 11:1–10: The Apostle Paul: Converted or Completed? 170
60. Romans 11:11–16: The Cheer I Can't Stop Chanting.................... 172
61. Romans 11:17–24: Halftime with the Apostle Paul 176
62. Romans 11:25–32: Why God Is Not Fair Is a Good Thing.............. 179
63. Week 9: Discussion Questions 183

Week 10: Romans 11:33–13:5

64. Romans 11:33–36: On Lighting Fires in the Sky...................... 187
65. Romans 12:1: The Jesus Manifesto................................... 189
66. Romans 12:2: Why the Mind Must Lead the Heart in the Matter of Transformation... 192
67. Romans 12:3–21: On Keeping the Cart Behind the Horse............. 194
68. Romans 13:1–3: Why We Must Pay Our Taxes 198
69. Romans 13:4–5: On Jesus, His Church, and the Government......... 200
70. Week 10: Discussion Questions.....................................204

Week 11: Romans 13:6–14:12

71. Romans 13:6–7: On Theology and Taxes 207
72. Romans 13:8–10: The Problem with Speed Limits and the Problem with Me. 210
73. Romans 13:11–14: Stop Hitting the Snooze Bar!...................... 213
74. Romans 14:1–4: Sweat the Small Stuff—and It's All Small Stuff 216
75. Romans 14:5–9: When the Conflict Is Not About the Conflict and What It Is Really About... 219

76. Romans 14:10–12: The Four Horsemen of the Apocalypse............222
77. Week 11: Discussion Questions 225

Week 12: Romans 14:13–15:22

78. Romans 14:13–18: Sometimes When You Are Right You Are Wrong 229
79. Romans 14:19–23: Yes, Our Relationships Are the Mission 231
80. Romans 15:1–4: Awakening Rides on the Rails of Friendship..........234
81. Romans 15:5–6: *Unus Christianus, Nullus Christianus*..................237
82. Romans 15:7–13: From Shepherding to Fishing 240
83. Romans 15:14–22: Ask Me About My Band 243
84. Week 12: Discussion Questions..................................248

Week 13: Romans 15:23–16:27

85. Romans 15:23–33: The Bond of a Band Versus the Rope of Sand.......251
86. Romans 16:1–2: Phoebe Was a Rock Star 254
87. Romans 16:3–16: Love Always Has a Name..........................256
88. Romans 16:17–19: A Closing Zinger................................259
89. Romans 16:20–24: Romans 16:19 Says..............................262
90. Romans 16:25–27: Now to Him 265
91. Week 13: Discussion Questions...................................268
    Conclusion 269

Preface

What are the two most important words of the day? I'm glad you asked. My take: the first word and the last word. Who gets the first word in your day? Who gets the last word? I have a confession: I have realized my slow drift into giving Instagram the first word of my day. It was simple and benign—just a quick scroll through the photos my friends posted over the last half day or so. Then this realization: Netflix was getting the last word of my day. Before drifting off to sleep, I would watch the next episode of some show that had caught my attention along the way. First word: *Instagram*. Last word: *Netflix*.

Days become weeks. Weeks become months. Months become years. And days, weeks, months, and years become us. Our lives consist not in the big decisions and banner events dotting our calendars but in the little things we consistently do day after day after day. We are what we do . . . every single day.

Each one of us has within our stewardship the ability to decide who will get the first and last words in our life. You know where this is headed. But first let me tell you what happened with my Instagram-Netflix ways. The problem is that I want to make Instagram and Netflix the problem when they aren't the problem. The problem is with me and the misspent priority of my own heart. So I didn't decide to delete Instagram and swear off Netflix. Instead, I decided I would shift the priority of my heart. I determined to give the Word of God the first word and the last word of my days.

Though my day may be filled with a thousand distractions and a hundred course corrections, it is now determined—my day will be framed by, surrounded with, enclosed in the Word of God. First Word. Last Word. God's Word.

> The grass withers and the flowers fall,
> but the word of our God endures forever.
> (Isaiah 40:8)

Consider the stark simplicity and brazen boldness of this word from the prophet Isaiah. Everything is ephemeral. Only one thing is eternal—the Word of God.

Next to the front door of our home, the one we enter and exit through almost every time, is a chalkboard. And on the chalkboard are written those words. I read that verse at least once every single day. I say it aloud so my ears can hear it. Can I possibly be reminded enough that everything around me is passing away save one thing—the Word of God? Can I possibly be encouraged enough to come to Jesus and have him build my life on the singular enduring reality of the Word of God? First Word. Last Word. God's Word.

I offer you an invitation through this book to journey with me and others to shift the priority of your heart and mind. Each day we will gather around a biblical text. We will invite the text of Scripture to speak both the first and the last word of our day. Write some of the text for the day in a journal or on a notecard, a whiteboard, or a chalkboard, and make it a simple act of worship to read it aloud each morning as the first word of the day and also at the close as the last word of the day.

Along the way we will reflect together on how to increase the priority, prominence, and integration of the Word of God in our everyday lives. If we will give ourselves to the gentle work of this way of walking together, I suspect we will find pathways of delight and devotion winding through the wilderness of this world and the sanctuaries of our own souls that we never imagined existed. And something tells me these First-Word-Last-Word-God's-Word paths will find their way into tomorrow and next week and next month and onward, until they have become our lives.

Now I'm going to say, "The grass withers and the flowers fall," and you are going to say, "But the word of our God endures forever."

J. D. WALT

How This Works

This is a different kind of Bible study. The Bible is both the source and the subject. And you will learn information about the Bible along the way, such as its history, context, original languages, and authors. The goal is not educational in nature, but transformational. We will focus more on knowing Jesus than on knowing *about* Jesus.

To that end, each reading begins with the definitive inspiration of the Holy Spirit, the ongoing, unfolding text of Scripture. Following that is a short and hopefully substantive insight into the text and some aspect of its meaning. For insight to lead to deeper influence, we turn the text into prayer. Finally, influence must run its course toward impact. This is why you will find questions at the end of each chapter. These questions are designed not to elicit information but to crystallize intention.

Discipleship always leads from inspiration to attention, from attention to intention, and from intention to action.

Committing to Everyday Reading and Prayer

While Scripture always addresses us personally, it is not written to us individually. The content of Scripture cries out for a community of listeners and readers. This resource is designed for discipleship in community. You could read this like a traditional book—a few pages or chapters at a time. You could cram the readings the night before a group meeting. Those ways of reading are not the intention of this book. Keep in mind, Daily Seeds is not called *Daily* Seeds for kicks. We believe Scripture is worthy of our most focused and consistent attention. Every day. We all have misses, but let's make everyday reading and prayer more than a noble aspiration; let's make it our covenant with one another.

This discipleship tool will create spiritual habits of individual reading and of praying the biblical text—six days on your own and one day with others.

How to Use with Small Groups

Daily Seeds is a proven discipleship resource that works in a variety of contexts—from churches studying a book of the Bible together to small groups to Sunday school classes to virtual meetings. Assuming your group meets weekly, group and class members should read one chapter every day. You will notice there is not an assigned reading for the seventh day. On the seventh day, meet with your group to share, pray, and encourage one another with insights or struggles that the text brought up in you during the previous six days. Use the following guidelines to help structure your group meetings as you allow Scripture to transform you in community.

The guidelines for using Daily Seeds in small groups or class settings are meant to be simple. Perhaps share the responsibility of leading group meetings. Remember that the goal is transformation.

1. Hearing the Text
Invite the group to settle into silence for a period of no less than one and no more than five minutes. Ask an appointed person to keep time and to read the biblical text covering the period of days since the last group meeting. Allow at least one minute of silence following the reading of the text.

2. Responding to the Text
Invite anyone from the group to respond to the reading by answering these prompts: What did you hear? What did you see? What did you otherwise sense from the Lord?

3. Sharing Insights and Implications for Discipleship
Moving in an orderly rotation (or free-for-all), invite people to share insights and implications from the week's readings. What did you find challenging, encouraging, provocative, comforting, invasive, inspiring,

corrective, affirming, guiding, or warning? Allow group conversation to proceed at will. Limit to one sharing item per turn, with multiple rounds of discussion.

4. Shaping Intentions for Prayer

Invite each person in the group to share a single discipleship intention for the week ahead. It is helpful if this goal for growing in discipleship can also be framed as a question the group can use to check in from the prior week. At each person's turn, they are invited to share how their intention went during the previous week. The class or group can open and close the meeting according to its established patterns.

Introduction

Dear Christian,

I've got a question for you: What is Romans?

The obvious answer might be, "It's a book of the Bible."

Well, yes and no. Romans is not actually a book but a letter.

Then you say, "It is a letter, but this letter is a book of the Bible." Then I say, "Maybe that's part of the problem with our approach to Romans."

Now you think I'm quibbling, but bear with me. When someone brings up a book, we ask, "What is the book about?" But when someone mentions receiving a letter, we ask, "What did it say?" This is more than nuance here. Stay with me.

A book is written by an author to a reader.

A letter is written by a sender to a recipient.

A book assumes an audience.

A letter assumes a relationship.

Some of the issue with how we have read and approached Romans comes from our seeing Romans primarily as a book. We have approached it as a book of doctrine or something of a theological treatise on the finer points of divine salvation. And as we tend to do with books, we go in one of two directions. We write a much longer book about the book in question, or we try to write a much shorter version of the book in question. In the former case, we have encyclopedic-length commentaries on the "book" of Romans. In the latter case, we have the so-called TL;DR (Too Long; Didn't Read—i.e., CliffsNotes) versions. The most succinct version distills the whole book—even the whole plan of salvation—into four verses from the whole text (a.k.a. "The Romans Road").

"And so," you are thinking, "this guy is telling me we don't need more books about letters in his book about a letter." That leads me to point out that this introduction is formatted as a letter. I don't want you to see this document as a traditional book. I want you to see it as a series of letters—over ninety of them! They are letters from me to you, flowing from the letter of all letters—Paul's letter to the Romans.

I want you to see it this way because it's the actual truth of how this volume came to be. For the past ten years, every single day, I have written a letter to a growing group of people all over the world who have one thing in common: We are following Jesus into the great awakening movement he calls his church. The daily letter begins with a prayer of consecration, focuses in on an unfolding text of Scripture (for example, Romans), engages the text with our everyday life, and ends with a prayer for transformation or deliverance or whatever the Spirit calls for on that particular day. For those who listen to the letter in the audio format (a.k.a. the podcast), we sing one of the great hymns of the church together (and yes, I lead the singing—a capella). The whole thing is called the Wake-Up Call, and I would love for you to join us at seedbed.com/wakeupcall/.

Meanwhile, one day, to my great joy, I learned that the publishing team at Zondervan Reflective was receiving and reading these daily letters. And as letters do, they build and strengthen relationships. They reached out to me and wanted me to share these letters with the likes of you, and that's the story of how my letters have been bound into this "book."

So what is Romans?

It is a letter founded in and flowing from relationships—Paul's relationship with Jesus and Paul's relationship with a tiny church in the ancient megacity of Rome. This unique and powerful set of relationships, of course, is called the church. And to help us journey into and through this letter, I have written you over ninety letters flowing from our relationship with Jesus and our emerging relationships with each other, which are already multiplying and growing. So how about I end this introductory letter and open up the next one. Let me close in the way I open every letter every day on the Wake-Up Call:

Wake up, sleeper, rise from the dead, and Christ will shine on you. (Ephesians 5:14)

For the awakening,

JOHN DAVID (J. D.) WALT JR.
Founder and Sower in Chief
Seedbed, Inc.

1
WEEK

Romans 1:1–2:4

WEEK

1

Romans 1:2–4

Romans 1:1–7

1 | What Is Your Calling?

> Paul, a servant of Christ Jesus, called to be an apostle and set apart for the gospel of God—the gospel he promised beforehand through his prophets in the Holy Scriptures regarding his Son, who as to his earthly life was a descendant of David, and who through the Spirit of holiness was appointed the Son of God in power by his resurrection from the dead: Jesus Christ our Lord. Through him we received grace and apostleship to call all the Gentiles to the obedience that comes from faith for his name's sake. And you also are among those Gentiles who are called to belong to Jesus Christ.
>
> To all in Rome who are loved by God and called to be his holy people:
>
> Grace and peace to you from God our Father and from the Lord Jesus Christ.

Consider This

What is your calling? People expend so much energy, throughout their lives, trying to figure out exactly what their calling is. We tend to think it is a specific career or vocation or some particular job. Many spend much of their lives feeling as though they have missed their calling. They feel stuck in a job they can do but don't love. More challenging, they spend a lot of time wondering if God wants them to be doing something other than what they are presently doing—like maybe they are supposed to go into "the ministry." College students live in enormous anxiety about needing to figure out what they are going to do with their lives before they graduate. I regularly tell my own collegiate children to relax—even Jesus didn't get started until he was thirty.

I've got good news for all of you. You don't need to figure out your calling. It's already set in stone. Did you catch it in today's text? It is right there in verse 6.

> You ... are called to belong to Jesus Christ.

This is your full-time vocation. It is your 100 percent job 100 percent of the time. You are called to belong to Jesus Christ. He tells us who we are and why we are here. Every possible question and quandary in life can be answered if approached from this singular starting place. It's why I want you to begin in a place of consecration every single day with the words *Jesus, I belong to you*. Promise me you will never, ever, ever skip that. Yesterday's consecration is not sufficient for today's calling.

Our calling must include and inform our jobs or careers, but it is much larger and far more comprehensive than our workweek. That's why the whole concept of retirement is an absurdity in the kingdom of Jesus. Calling transcends retirement. Sure, you can quit your job, but you can't retire from your calling. In fact, I call the years between the ages of sixty and eighty the "kingdom prime." And over eighty is "kingdom superprime."

I once heard a Mother Teresa story I will never forget. A young adult showed up at Mother Teresa's convent to work with lepers. He was put in a back office processing documents and records. Very unhappy, the man somehow got to Mother with his grievance. He said to her, "Mother, I came here from across the world to work with lepers, and all I am doing here is paperwork. My calling is to serve lepers." She lovingly yet sternly replied, "Son, your calling is not to serve lepers. Your calling is to belong to Jesus. Now get back to the paperwork."

The Prayer

Jesus, we belong to you. Yes, Jesus, I belong to you. From this place we can go many places, but until we get to this place, though we may go everywhere, we will have gone nowhere. Jesus, open up the message and the meaning of this ancient letter—perhaps the most significant letter ever written in the history of the world. Take us to Rome and then translate Rome to our home. And yes, Jesus, you are our home for that is what it means to belong to you. Praying in your name. Amen.

The Questions

Jesus I belong to you (. ? !) How do you punctuate that sentence in your life—with a period, a question mark, an exclamation mark, a comma? Say more.

2 Romans 1:8–15
Give Me 100

> First, I thank my God through Jesus Christ for all of you, because your faith is being reported all over the world. God, whom I serve in my spirit in preaching the gospel of his Son, is my witness how constantly I remember you in my prayers at all times; and I pray that now at last by God's will the way may be opened for me to come to you.
>
> I long to see you so that I may impart to you some spiritual gift to make you strong—that is, that you and I may be mutually encouraged by each other's faith. I do not want you to be unaware, brothers and sisters, that I planned many times to come to you (but have been prevented from doing so until now) in order that I might have a harvest among you, just as I have had among the other Gentiles.
>
> I am obligated both to Greeks and non-Greeks, both to the wise and the foolish. That is why I am so eager to preach the gospel also to you who are in Rome.

Consider This

Can we get our bearings a bit on what is going on here?

First-century Rome was the capital of the world. It was a city of around a million people. The early church in Rome, not to be confused with the modern-day Basilica of St. Peter in the Vatican, was a series of house churches likely comprising about one hundred people.

Get this fixed in your mind: We are in the most powerful city in the first-century world, ruled over by the most powerful (and cruel) man in the world, Lord Caesar (Nero). The threat is a hundred lower-class people scattered across the city (meeting in homes) who are ostensibly being led by a dead man who was reportedly resurrected from the grave and ascended to heaven and sitteth at the right hand of God the Father Almighty, Lord Messiah (Jesus).

It gets better. We are reading a letter written by the apostle Paul around the year 50ish to a tiny church planted by the apostle Peter several years earlier. Behold what is unfolding:

> First, I thank my God through Jesus Christ for all of you, because your faith is being reported all over the world.

The faith of a hundred people was being reported all over the world, and they didn't even have the internet. By the power of the gospel of Jesus, through the obedience of their faith, one hundred people—bound by love and federated by freedom—would plant the flag of the kingdom of God in such a way that the Roman Empire would ultimately come undone at the seams.

Maybe that's why John Wesley would write centuries later in the midst of the British Great Awakening, "Give me one hundred preachers who fear nothing but sin and desire nothing but God, and I care not whether they be clergymen or laymen, they alone will shake the gates of Hell and set up the kingdom of Heaven upon Earth."[1]

This letter to the one hundred Christians in the several little Roman house churches is easily one of the most important letters ever written in the history of the world—not because of what it says to us but what it said to them. For today, my friends, we are them. And Rome is now another name for home. Our ten-year-olds are killing themselves at epidemic rates. Our schools have become slaughterhouses. The Democrats and the Republicans and the seductive, toxic politics of outrage will not save the day. Only Jesus can.

---

1. John Wesley, writing at age 87 to Alexander Mather, quoted in Luke Tyerman, *The Life and Times of the Rev. John Wesley* (London: Hodder and Stoughton, 1871), III:632.

That is the message of the letter to the Romans and to us. The gospel of the kingdom of Jesus is the simple yet comprehensive solution for all that is broken in our lives and in the world.

In the first century in a city of a million, the faith of a hundred was being reported all over the world. Not so long ago, in this the twenty-first century, we witnessed the faith of nineteen college students light the first fires of great awakening in this century at Asbury University. And I do not exaggerate when I say their faith was reported all over the world.[2]

The Prayer

Jesus, we belong to you. Yes, Jesus, I belong to you. I am in awe of you and what you can do through the simple obedience of faith. Would you awaken this kind of faith in me? I confess I think I grasp what it means, but I likely have no idea. I offer you my beginner's mind. Teach me. Train me. Open the eyes of my heart. Enliven the hope of my spirit by your Spirit. We are in need of awakening. We are desperate for you. Praying in Jesus's name. Amen.

The Questions

What could happen if we woke up and began to move in the obedience of faith? Can you remember a time when you moved by faith in response to some way Jesus was leading you or your family or church? What happened? What is happening?

---

2. Thomas Lyons, "When a Christian Revival Goes Viral," *The Atlantic*, February 23, 2023, https://www.theatlantic.com/ideas/archive/2023/02/asbury-kentucky-university-christian-revival/673176/.

Romans 1:16–17

3   How to Have a Blessed Life

> *For I am not ashamed of the gospel, because it is the power of God that brings salvation to everyone who believes: first to the Jew, then to the Gentile. For in the gospel the righteousness of God is revealed—a righteousness that is by faith from first to last, just as it is written: "The righteous will live by faith."*

Consider This

Today's text is nothing short of a burning bush—on fire and consuming but not consumed. It has burned with brilliance from the day it was inspired by the Holy Spirit and written on parchment.

Billions have warmed to its fire and been found in its light. If a summary of Romans could be written (which it can't), this passage is it.

I don't know if you know this about me, but I am a poet. I just decided one day many years hence. Back around Easter 2023 I wrote the following poem after meeting up with an old friend. While I know my verse will not do the text justice, I am certain my normal commentary is wholly inadequate. I call it . . .

The Hard and Beautiful Truth

> "I don't want you to think I'm not a good person."
> That's what my old friend said to me
> upon meeting again after decades apart
> and a long confession of her broken story.
> I assured her with The Hard and Beautiful Truth:
> "You are not a good person.
> I'm not either.
> We are broken sinners."
> Something deep in me (and maybe you too)
> wants to believe we are good, or worse that we are bad—

that we just need to lose twenty pounds,
drop a few bad habits, and try harder to be better.
Then I assure myself with The Hard and Beautiful Truth:
Good people and bad people is a lie
from the pit of hell,
and the way from good to great (or bad to worse)
paves the way there.
Jesus only goes from
Death to Life
Lost to Found
Slave to Free
Broken to Beautiful
Then she asked me, "If you are not good, what are you?"
"LOVED," I said.
"I am loved,
and you are too."

> For I am not ashamed of the gospel, because it is the power of God that brings salvation to everyone who believes: first to the Jew, then to the Gentile. For in the gospel the righteousness of God is revealed—a righteousness that is by faith from first to last, just as it is written: "The righteous will live by faith."

The Prayer

Jesus, we belong to you. Yes, Jesus, I belong to you. And you belong to me. I am so weary of trying to fake goodness and appear better than I am. Who am I fooling besides myself? Wake me up to the beautiful truth that nothing bad I have done renders me worthless and nothing good I have done renders me worthy. Jesus, while I was a sinner you died for me. You love me. I just want to keep saying it—You love me! You love me! You love me!—until the sad tears become happy tears and all is well with my soul. So I say I love you and I love you and I love you. Praying in your name, Jesus. Amen.

The Questions

How about you? Tired of the good person–bad person calculus of hell? Ready for the gospel? Jesus is.

Romans 1:18–23

4

From a Burning Bush to a Burning House

> *The wrath of God is being revealed from heaven against all the godlessness and wickedness of people, who suppress the truth by their wickedness, since what may be known about God is plain to them, because God has made it plain to them. For since the creation of the world God's invisible qualities—his eternal power and divine nature—have been clearly seen, being understood from what has been made, so that people are without excuse.*
>
> *For although they knew God, they neither glorified him as God nor gave thanks to him, but their thinking became futile and their foolish hearts were darkened. Although they claimed to be wise, they became fools and exchanged the glory of the immortal God for images made to look like a mortal human being and birds and animals and reptiles.*

Consider This

Chapter 1 of Romans takes us on quite a journey.

Yesterday we stood together in awe of the burning bush of the New Testament. Today and tomorrow we will stand in shock before a burning house.

The burning bush:

> For I am not ashamed of the gospel, because it is the power of God that brings salvation to everyone who believes: first to the Jew, then to the Gentile. For in the gospel the righteousness of

> God is revealed—a righteousness that is by faith from first to last, just as it is written: "The righteous will live by faith."

The burning house:

> The wrath of God is being revealed from heaven against all the godlessness and wickedness of people, who suppress the truth by their wickedness.

The real dilemma we must solve here at the outset—as it relates not only to the letter to the Romans but to our very hearts, homes, churches, and cities—is this one: Where will we focus? Will we focus on the burning house or the burning bush? Will we focus on the problem of sin or the power of the gospel? Will we focus on the crucified, risen Messiah or the chaotic mess in the world and our lives? Will we focus on the diabolical problem of sin and its myriad manifestations or the singular solution of salvation in Jesus Christ?

The seduction is to think you can choose both. To try and choose both is to choose neither. It is to wind up stuck in the eddies instead of the river (i.e., Romans 7 versus Romans 8). We will not deny sin here. We must not. Sin is undeniably real. It is diabolical and devastating, and yet it is a distraction. Sin's most deceptive and successful strategy is to consume the conversation and crowd Jesus out. We can't deny sin's reality. But we must deny sin our focus. We must reserve our unfettered and undeniable focus for Jesus himself, only, ever, and always.

The Prayer

Jesus, we belong to you. Yes, Jesus, I belong to you. As we enter into the abyss of sin, we want to fix our eyes on you. We are sinners, which is to say we are profoundly susceptible to distraction and deception. We want salvation, not just a little bit but comprehensively. We know this salvation will not come by focusing on sin and trying to defeat it but by being fixed on Jesus, who has defeated sin, and on belonging to him—believing more, beholding deeper, and thereby becoming completely his. Come, Holy Spirit, and prepare the way for the Lord Jesus like never before. Praying in his name. Amen.

=== The Questions ===

Do you find yourself wanting to talk more about sin—in yourself, in other people, in the chaotic broken world around us—than about Jesus and the comprehensive solution of salvation?

Romans 1:24-32

5
The Difference Between Our Sins and Our Sin

> Therefore God gave them over in the sinful desires of their hearts to sexual impurity for the degrading of their bodies with one another. They exchanged the truth about God for a lie, and worshiped and served created things rather than the Creator—who is forever praised. Amen.
>
> Because of this, God gave them over to shameful lusts. Even their women exchanged natural sexual relations for unnatural ones. In the same way the men also abandoned natural relations with women and were inflamed with lust for one another. Men committed shameful acts with other men, and received in themselves the due penalty for their error.
>
> Furthermore, just as they did not think it worthwhile to retain the knowledge of God, so God gave them over to a depraved mind, so that they do what ought not to be done. They have become filled with every kind of wickedness, evil, greed and depravity. They are full of envy, murder, strife, deceit and malice. They are gossips, slanderers, God-haters, insolent, arrogant and boastful; they invent ways of doing evil; they disobey their parents; they have no understanding, no fidelity, no love, no mercy. Although they know God's righteous decree that those who do such things deserve death, they not only continue to do these very things but also approve of those who practice them.

Consider This

Let me say at the outset that I believe every single word of this text without exception (and every passage of Scripture, for that matter). It is a clear, unambiguous strafing of both capital-S Sin and lowercase-s sins and the people who commit them. And to be clear, that is all of us—every single one.

But I want to practice what I preach and give prior focus to the gospel about which this entire book (if not the entire Bible) is devoted. It is essential to understand that the gospel does not begin with sin but with God. So many theological frameworks of the last five hundred years make sin their starting place. The Bible does not begin with Genesis 3 but with Genesis 1 and 2. Note well how Romans follows the same pattern. Paul begins with the gospel and even the strong allusion to creation (Genesis 1-2 via Romans 1:20) before delving into the abyss of the fall (Genesis 3) and all the darkness it has led to. In Romans 1:24–32, Paul captures the very essence (if not the definition) of Sin in one sentence. I capitalized Sin here intentionally. I will say more about this later, but we must begin to grasp the relationship between our Sin and our sins. Paul begins by giving us one of the clearest definitions of capital-S Sin in the whole Bible:

> They exchanged the truth about God for a lie, and worshiped and served created things rather than the Creator—who is forever praised. Amen.

Paul then gives us a representative but not an exhaustive list of the little-s sins by detailing for us the scene of an average day in first-century Rome (and any other society suffering in the advanced stages of the metastatic cancer of Sin). Our sins are the symptoms, but the sickness is Sin. The rest of the letter and every other letter in the New Testament is all about the cure. It comes down to one Word: *Jesus*.

We must make a critical shift in our understanding and orientation before launching into the deeps of this letter to the Romans and to us. We must shift from the notion of the little phrase "the gospel of Jesus" to the equally little but infinitely larger phrase: The gospel *is* Jesus.

I want you to reflect deeply on this today. The gospel is Jesus.

As Martin Luther famously sang, "He must win the battle." In fact, he already has.

The Prayer

Jesus, we belong to you. Yes, Jesus, I belong to you. You are the gospel. Teach me this. Holy Spirit, would you increase my understanding by first enlarging my curiosity around the meaning of this little phrase: Jesus is the gospel. In a world that is terminally ill with Sin cancer, I want to focus on the cure who is Jesus. I want to be cured of the disease of Sin and then healed from all the symptoms and the scar tissue left behind. Thank you, Jesus—so much. Thank you. Praying in your name. Amen.

The Questions

Do you see the distinction between "the gospel *of* Jesus" and "The gospel *is* Jesus"? Doodle and draft on that today in your heart, your mind, and your journal.

Romans 2:1-4

6   Reapproaching Repentance

> *You, therefore, have no excuse, you who pass judgment on someone else, for at whatever point you judge another, you are condemning yourself, because you who pass judgment do the same things. Now we know that God's judgment against those who do such things is based on truth. So when you, a mere human being, pass judgment on them and yet do the same things, do you think you will escape God's judgment? Or do you show contempt for the riches of his kindness, forbearance and patience, not realizing that God's kindness is intended to lead you to repentance?*

Consider This

I remember it like it was yesterday. It was the late 1900s, near the turn of the century, and I was a local church pastor in Texas. One day our worship leader invited me to listen to a new song he was writing. He wanted my thoughts. The song gripped me, and to remember it takes me there. Here are some of the words:

> It's your kindness, Lord
> That leads us to repentance.

My thoughts? Wow! Amazing! Perfect.

Though I had contributed thoughts and ideas to some of his other songs, I was speechless before this one.

The song revealed something about repentance I had never grasped. In those days repentance felt to me like behavior management. You know—stop sinning. If there were two words I would not have connected, they would have been *kindness* and *repentance*. And there they are plain as day in today's text:

> God's kindness is intended to lead you to repentance.

The Greek word behind "repentance" is *metanoia*.[3] It means to have a change of mindset. A related meaning for repentance is to make a 180-degree turnaround.

This brings us back around to our conversation about focus. Will we focus on the problem of Sin or on the person of Jesus? We can't simultaneously focus on that which we are turning away from and that which we are turning to. We must choose. The focus of repentance is not on turning away from sin but on turning to Jesus.

The person of Jesus is the riches of the kindness of God. As we turn to him, we begin to turn our lives over to him and sin loses not only

---

3. Andrew Dragos, "7 Things the Bible Teaches About Repentance," February 19, 2018, https://seedbed.com/7-things-the-bible-teaches-about-repentance/.

its luster but its power.[4] It's why the gospel is the power of God for the salvation of all who will believe. It's why the gospel is Jesus.

The Prayer

Jesus, we belong to you. Yes, Jesus, I belong to you. Jesus, you are the gospel. You are the kindness of God. You are the power of God. It's why I love to repent because it means turning to you. As I am turned to you, I cannot at the same time be turned to sin. Come Holy Spirit and train me in this turning to Jesus and turning my life over to him. It is an awe-filled thought to fathom how he has turned his life toward me. What a kindness. Praying in Jesus's name. Amen.

The Questions

What thoughts and images does the word *repentance* conjure in your mind and heart? Does this help you to reframe it by focusing on the one we are turning to?

---

4. Kenneth Collins, "Ken Collins on Wesley 24: The Repentance of Believers," November 15, 2015, https://seedbed.com/ken-collins-wesley-24/.

Week 1: Discussion Questions

Hearing the Text

Read Romans 1:1–2:4.

Responding to the Text

- What did you hear?
- What did you see?
- What did you otherwise sense from the Lord?

Sharing Insights and Implications for Discipleship

Drawing from the Scripture text and daily readings, what did you find challenging, encouraging, provocative, comforting, invasive, inspiring, corrective, affirming, guiding, or warning?

Shaping Intentions for Prayer

Write your discipleship intention for the week ahead.

Week 1:
Discussion Questions

Hearing the Text

Scripture: Luke

Responding to the Text

- What did you hear?
- What do you see?
- What did you otherwise experience in the text?

Sharing Insights and Implications for Discipleship

Drawing from the scripture text and daily readings, where did you find challenges with or insights for your active discipleship: nurturing, evangelizing, community-building, building up, or serving?

Shaping Intentions for Prayer

Write your discipleship intention for the week ahead.

2
WEEK

Romans 2:5–3:18

Romans 2:5–11

8 | Sin Swamp: Got to Go Through It

> But because of your stubbornness and your unrepentant heart, you are storing up wrath against yourself for the day of God's wrath, when his righteous judgment will be revealed. God "will repay each person according to what they have done." To those who by persistence in doing good seek glory, honor and immortality, he will give eternal life. But for those who are self-seeking and who reject the truth and follow evil, there will be wrath and anger. There will be trouble and distress for every human being who does evil: first for the Jew, then for the Gentile; but glory, honor and peace for everyone who does good: first for the Jew, then for the Gentile. For God does not show favoritism.

Consider This

I remember as a kid being led through the follow-the-leader type exercise called "The Bear Hunt." The leader would speak and make hand gestures, and the kids would follow suit.

"We're going on a bear hunt." (kids repeat)
"We come to a swamp." (kids repeat)
"Can't go over it." (kids repeat)
"Can't go under it." (kids repeat)
"Can't go around it." (kids repeat)
"Got to go through it." (kids repeat)

This was followed by all manner of hand gestures and sound effects as we made our way through the swamp. Then we would come to the next obstacle and repeat the process.

Well, today we come to Sin Swamp, and we've got to go through it. There is no getting over, under, or around it. While sin is not creative, it is sophisticated. As a general principle, I maintain that our understanding of the gospel will go about as deep as our understanding of sin. We have already begun with some discussion on the difference between capital-S Sin and lowercase-s sins. We need to back up further now to get a better grasp of what sin even is.

So often I have heard sin defined as a willful transgression of a known law. I want to respond, "Okay, so now what?" This is to see sin primarily in a forensic or legal framework. I want us to understand it at a deeper level. You will remember last week we referenced the definition in Romans 1:25: "They exchanged the truth about God for a lie, and worshiped and served created things rather than the Creator."

Here's my take. Sin is the breaking of the singular commandment to "Love the Lord your God with all your heart and with all your soul and with all your mind and with all your strength" and to "Love your neighbor as yourself" (Mark 12:30–31).

Far beyond the concept of moral failure, sin is relational disintegration. It is the destruction of ourselves through the breaking of our relationship with God and the breakdown of our relationships with other people. It leads to the desecration of all of creation. It's why the opposite of sin is not morality or good behavior but love. Sin is the failure of human beings to love God, to love themselves in the way God loves them, and thereby the failure to love other people with the love of God.

This is a singular yet comprehensive failure, for to fail at any one of them is to fail at all of them. This is why sin, which is the failure of love, leads to the destruction of people, their relationships, and the creation we were commissioned to steward for God's glory.

This is why God hates sin: because sin destroys love.

And this, my friends, is where the wrath of God comes into the picture.[1] A wrathful God is not a rage-filled angry parent who wants to punish their children as though a payback would somehow solve the problem or prevent it from happening again. God's wrath is his righteous anger at anyone and anything that would desecrate and destroy his creation, especially his image bearers. This is the point of judgment and justice. This is why as members of the human race we are doomed.

God hates sin because sin destroys love. However, it does not follow that God hates sinners. This is the very essence of the gospel itself—God

---

1. See Sandra Richter, "Is Jesus More Loving Than God in the Old Testament," December 14, 2022, https://seedbed.com/is-jesus-more-loving-than-god-in-the-old-testament/.

loves sinners, and he would not only save them *from* sin but save them *for* glory. This is the point of mercy and grace. This is how as the human race we can be saved.

> But God demonstrates his own love for us in this: While we were still sinners, Christ died for us. Since we have now been justified by his blood, how much more shall we be saved from God's wrath through him! (Romans 5:8–9)

By the way, it looks like we will be days, if not weeks, here in Sin Swamp. Better get some extra bug spray.

The Prayer

Jesus, we belong to you. Yes, Jesus, I belong to you. Jesus, you are the gospel. I confess I have a way of trivializing sin. I also tend to think only of how sin affects me rather than about how it desecrates other people. I think of sin as my failure to act rightly rather than as my failure to love. Awaken me to reality such that I can understand the cost of my sin to others, to myself, and to you. Praying in Jesus's name. Amen.

The Questions

How does this way of understanding sin deepen your understanding of the gospel? How do you push back against it?

9 | Romans 2:12–16

On the Law, the Gospel, and the Religion of Weight Loss

> *All who sin apart from the law will also perish apart from the law, and all who sin under the law will be judged by the law. For it is not those who hear the law who are righteous in God's sight, but it is*

> those who obey the law who will be declared righteous. (Indeed, when Gentiles, who do not have the law, do by nature things required by the law, they are a law for themselves, even though they do not have the law. They show that the requirements of the law are written on their hearts, their consciences also bearing witness, and their thoughts sometimes accusing them and at other times even defending them.) This will take place on the day when God judges people's secrets through Jesus Christ, as my gospel declares.

Consider This

Welcome back to Sin Swamp where today we will be talking about the Law.

A text like today's seems irrelevant and even obtuse to the average twenty-first-century Bible reader. It feels like Paul is dealing with a first-century issue we no longer deal with. Truth is, we don't—and yet we do.

Just as there is capital-*S* Sin and little-*s* sins so there is the capital-*L* Law and all the little-*l* laws.

The capital-*L* Law, according to Jesus, is, "Love the Lord your God with all your heart and with all your soul and with all your mind and with all your strength" and "Love your neighbor as yourself" (Mark 12:30–31).

All the little-*l* laws show us examples of what it looks like to break the capital-*L* Law.

Capital-*S* Sin simply means the failure of love. Little-*s* sins are all the ways we do so. The problem is we put all the focus on the little-*l* laws and consequently the little-*s* sins. We must return our focus to the capital-*L* Law of love. Only this will shift us out of sin management mode with its endless behavior modification strategies, which is another name for religious legalism.

Let's bring it all together with a practical example.

It might surprise you to know I am obese. I'm not super fat, but according to the charts, I qualify. I am five foot eleven, and I weigh (can't believe I'm telling you this) 221 pounds as of the day I am writing. I have been stuck at 220 plus or minus for the past four years. I'm down from 236 pounds at my high. The charts say I should weigh around 180.

I've done calorie counting, WeightWatchers, Atkins, Whole30, keto, Mediterranean diet, intermittent fasting, macro management, diet pills, the Noom app, weight training, ten thousand steps a day, and whatever is next. Still, I remain obese—stuck at 220 pounds.

I find that all these programs and approaches have in common a focus on little-*l* laws and little-*s* sins. Don't do this, reduce that, measure this, count that, calories in, calories out, weigh every day, weigh every week, weight is just a number, don't weigh at all, throw the scale away, analyze, monitor, track, record, and repeat. And rest too, yes, rest. Oh yeah, and I forgot, drink a ton of water. The insane thing is that all of it kind of works and yet none of it really works at all. It is a kind of religion in and of itself.

Those are all just little-*l* laws, aren't they? And they all address little-*s* sins, don't they? More little laws will never get it done. And it's amazing how in focusing on so many things we miss the one thing. The whole point Paul will make about the Law and legalistic religion in Romans (and the rest of his letters) is that the law is powerless to change people. Sneak preview:

> For what the law was powerless to do because it was weakened by the flesh, God did by sending his own Son in the likeness of sinful flesh to be a sin offering. And so he condemned sin in the flesh, in order that the righteous requirement of the law might be fully met in us, who do not live according to the flesh but according to the Spirit. (Romans 8:3–4)

So how am I going to lose thirty to forty more pounds?

It's the wrong question, isn't it? That is the question of little laws and little sins.

So what is the right question?

Some of you are undoubtedly asking, What does any of this have to do with Jesus and Romans and being a Christian? What does my physical body have to do with being more spiritually alive and mature? What if the answer is—everything?

Here's another sneak peek:

Therefore, I urge you, brothers and sisters, in view of God's mercy, to offer your **bodies** as a living sacrifice, holy and pleasing to God—this is your true and proper worship. (Romans 12:1, emphasis added)

What if the question is, "How might I offer my body as a living sacrifice, holy and pleasing to God?" Every. Single. Day. That would mean asking this kind of question:

How might I love God with my body?

From here we might ask this question: "How might I live according to the Spirit and not according to the flesh?"

Now we are getting somewhere.

The Prayer

Jesus, we belong to you. Yes, Jesus, I belong to you. Jesus, you are the gospel. I find myself wanting to throw off all the rules and regulations and simply abandon myself to you, to be embraced by you, to receive freedom from you, to behold you, yes, to love you with everything I've got, even my body. Something tells me this deeper love of you is the way to the deepest practical life change. I can't quite grasp it, but I'm beginning to get it. Praying in your name, Jesus. Amen.

The Questions

How are you sifting through what I'm trying to sort out here? Does my use of the weight problem analogy inspire you or infuriate you? Could Jesus have something to do with bodily health? Could he have everything to do with it?

Romans 2:17–24

10   A Diatribe Against Self-Righteous Sinners

> Now you, if you call yourself a Jew; if you rely on the law and boast in God; if you know his will and approve of what is superior because you are instructed by the law; if you are convinced that you are a guide for the blind, a light for those who are in the dark, an instructor of the foolish, a teacher of little children, because you have in the law the embodiment of knowledge and truth—you, then, who teach others, do you not teach yourself? You who preach against stealing, do you steal? You who say that people should not commit adultery, do you commit adultery? You who abhor idols, do you rob temples? You who boast in the law, do you dishonor God by breaking the law? As it is written: "God's name is blasphemed among the Gentiles because of you."

Consider This

Paul engages today in the practice of a diatribe. Permit me a bit of a diatribe in that same spirit.

The deeper purpose of the Law is to make us deeply aware of our need for God so that we have some possibility of actually obeying it. I once heard a great man of God say, "The Law was given so that the Spirit might be desired, and the Spirit was given so that the Law might be obeyed." Reflect deeply on this truth.

The problem is the way broken human beings tend to approach the Law with a "yes, we can" attitude. Show me the rules, and I'll show you a rule keeper. Show me a rule keeper, and I'll show you a moralist, which is someone who endlessly judges other people. Something in us wants to justify ourselves—to show we have the heart, mind, soul, and strength to do it ourselves. And then we want to hold others to this same standard. There is a word for this: *self-righteousness*—which is the world of honor and shame, of pride and pretense, of virtue signaling and cancel culture. It is alive and well in religious and irreligious communities alike.

Obey the rules and you are in. Disobey the rules and you are out. Disobey the rules while hiding behind your enforcement of the same rules on others, and we will make you a leader in the community. These kinds of leaders killed Jesus. And these kinds of leaders are still among us. Their way of life continues to do violence to Jesus, all while they think they are doing him a favor. And yes, our churches are full of them. They are called hypocrites. The capital-*H* Hypocrites are the leaders and the little-*h* hypocrites are the followers, but from the first century to the twenty-first, they are all the same.

One of the telltale signs you are dealing with a legalistic, hypocritical leader is they are always trying to control the narrative, which makes them impervious to correction—always finding fault and never owning it. In these communities, repentance is behavioral modification rather than relational realignment. And repentance is image management rather than identity reorientation.

Paul knows these people because he was one of them, and in today's text he starts by sparring with them and then he takes off the gloves. He identifies them as the problem. He basically says the hypocrisy in the church is the cause of the unbelief in the world.

> You who boast in the law, do you dishonor God by breaking the law? As it is written: "God's name is blasphemed among the Gentiles because of you."

And in the tradition of Jesus, Isaiah likens such so-called righteousness to filthy rags (see Isaiah 64:6). Religious systems are notoriously deployed in the service of image management. The gospel is about a total renovation of one's identity. Jesus hates image management. He only cares about deep identity formation. It's why his gospel is about the righteousness that comes from faith from first to last.

The problem is how a warning to hypocrites never actually gets to them because they are ingrained to think you must be talking about somebody else. So I think what I am saying here is could you be open to the fact that I may be talking to you?

The Prayer

Jesus, we belong to you. Jesus, I belong to you. Jesus, you are the gospel. I want to open my mind and heart to you. I confess, I often want to appear better than I actually am, which is to say I want to manage my image. Thank you that you will not deal with my image—only my deep identity. Would you come in and completely renovate my identity so that I might be remade in your image—to be a real, true, just, and merciful human being? That looks and feels like freedom to me. Come, Holy Spirit. Praying in Jesus's name. Amen.

The Questions

What resonates with you today? What offends you? Do you or have you seen these kinds of sin patterns in other people and communities? Identify without judging. ;0)

Romans 2:25–29

11   The Butterflied Heart

> *Circumcision has value if you observe the law, but if you break the law, you have become as though you had not been circumcised. So then, if those who are not circumcised keep the law's requirements, will they not be regarded as though they were circumcised? The one who is not circumcised physically and yet obeys the law will condemn you who, even though you have the written code and circumcision, are a lawbreaker.*
>
> *A person is not a Jew who is one only outwardly, nor is circumcision merely outward and physical. No, a person is a Jew who is one inwardly; and circumcision is circumcision of the heart, by the Spirit, not by the written code. Such a person's praise is not from other people, but from God.*

Consider This

The bottom line of chapter 2 is the ground is level at the foot of the cross. Jew or gentile—a sinner is a sinner is a sinner, and we are all one of them. Stop comparing. Stop judging. Stop faking. Today Paul drops a bomb of a hint about all the goodness to come. The hint comes in this stunning phrase, a heretofore uncombined combination of words:

> circumcision of the heart, by the Spirit

So think about circumcision (and I'll spare you the graphic details). Now think about the heart, which Paul poignantly chooses as a metaphor. Now think about the Holy Spirit. Circumcision of the heart by the Spirit.

Now, besides everything, what did circumcision mean to the Jews? It was the mark of belonging to God. The circumcised heart is the mark of belonging to Jesus. It is not a mark made by human hands but by the Holy Spirit. I see it as the cauterizing of the cross.

I got an interesting text message from a friend. It was in response to the entry where I was super real about my body and losing weight. Here is the thread:

Friend: Dear Jesus, turn my heart into a fillet of surrender. Today.
Me: What do you mean by fillet?
Friend: I had a dream years ago that my heart was split like a fillet and all these butterflies came flying out and they all went different ways to do good things for Jesus and I was so peaceful. I still envision it and feel like all is well.
Friend: I guess it's more like butterflying meat. Which (to me) brings it a step deeper.
Me: The Bible calls what you are referring to as the circumcision of the heart—which signifies the kind of surrender you are referring to—which releases the kind of flourishing you describe with the butterflies.
Friend: PS to John David, get rid of the scale.

I know many of you want this very thing for your life too. And you know what? Jesus knows it too. He sees your heart and it pleases him. I asked him if he would speak to you today, by his Spirit, through my yielded heart and free-flowing words. I am asking Jesus to circumcise your heart by his Spirit right here and right now. Here's my sense of his word to you today:

My Daughter, My Son,

 I see you and I delight in you greatly. I don't want anything from you. I am not looking for you to do something for me. I am not needing you to try to become someone for me. I simply want you, the real, deep, true you—not the person you think you should be or the one you hoped you would become by now, or even the one you take pride in having become. I want the you who you were when you were a child before it all became so complicated and broken and many other things it was never meant to be. Bring me your heart now that it might be circumcised by my Spirit—butterflied, laid open, and made whole again.

 I want you to let all the broken past be finally buried now, as in a grave, my grave, where I can cut it away like the lesions it has become on your soul, compromising and often crushing your true identity. I will give back your wounds as resurrected scars of glory. I'll give back your ashes as resurrected beauty. I'll give back your canceled sins as stories of salvation. I'll give back your brokenness as resurrected blessedness. All of this suffering I will give back to you as a song you will sing to me for the rest of your days until the day you sing it before me face-to-face.

 And I'm not looking for the you of your achievements and accolades and accomplishments—the you that you clamor for others to see. I want you to put all that on the shelf, my shelf, and let me cut away the broken attachments to your heart and heal the distortions they have done to your soul. I simply want you, like a child who can be held, carried, embraced, and blessed for nothing but love. I will give back your insecurities as the mighty fortress of my safe and secure presence. I'll give back your achievements in the form of my affirmation over your deepest identity, which has nothing to do with your performance. I'll give back your trophies, stripped of their idolatry and resurrected from the dead, as tokens of my glory you will one day lay at my feet again.

Give me your heart, in full surrender, fuller than ever before. Trust me completely and with abandon. Find your knees, make an altar, and do whatever it takes to mark these moments, for these are the moments I am marking you. I am writing my name on your heart again. And I know you may have done this before, and you will certainly do it again. What's important is you do it now, right now, bringing your heart just as you are. No expectation. No anticipation. Feeling it or not, willing or willful. Just bring a pure, unbridled, unconditional gift of your deepest heart to me in love. You belong to me. I belong to you. This is love, and you will never be the same again.

The Prayer

Jesus, we belong to you. Jesus, I belong to you. Jesus, you are the gospel—the pure, unadulterated, too good to be true but true goodness of God. I not only believe you today, but I receive you. I receive you in greater measure than ever before. I want the circumcision of the heart by the Spirit. I sense it will be costly and yet nowhere near as costly as a life lived without it. Holy Spirit, lead me into this deep place with Jesus anew and afresh. This will be awakening. Praying in Jesus's name. Amen.

The Questions

Did you enter into this prayer of the circumcision of the heart today? What happened? What is happening? What holds you back?

Romans 3:1–8

12 | Before Jesus Lifts, Jesus Levels

> What advantage, then, is there in being a Jew, or what value is there in circumcision? Much in every way! First of all, the Jews have been entrusted with the very words of God.
>
> What if some were unfaithful? Will their unfaithfulness nullify God's faithfulness? Not at all! Let God be true, and every human being a liar. As it is written:
>
> > "So that you may be proved right when you speak
> > and prevail when you judge."
>
> But if our unrighteousness brings out God's righteousness more clearly, what shall we say? That God is unjust in bringing his wrath on us? (I am using a human argument.) Certainly not! If that were so, how could God judge the world? Someone might argue, "If my falsehood enhances God's truthfulness and so increases his glory, why am I still condemned as a sinner?" Why not say—as some slanderously claim that we say—"Let us do evil that good may result"? Their condemnation is just!

===== Consider This =====

I'm not going to lie. Romans is hard. Today's text is hard to make heads or tails of for me. I get the feeling someone has lawyered up and is asking the kinds of questions a person asks when they don't understand (or don't like) what's being discussed. They are the questions of a religious person whose heart is not right. They are the questions of a person who doesn't really want answers but rather wants to play the part of an agitator. It's kind of like when people don't want to hear what you are trying to say so they ask ridiculous questions that obfuscate the whole conversation. It's kind of like those people in the Bible study who never do the homework and instead of being quiet, they try to convince everyone of their intelligence by releasing their pet rabbits into the room so others might give chase.

It is difficult to deal with uber-religious people on the one hand and recently converted pagan heathens on the other. Maybe I'm missing it, but that's how I'm sizing up the scene here in Rome. And the truth is, these two groups don't get along. It's a judgment-fest. It's kind of like the scene in the movie *The Jesus Revolution* when the pastor's daughter invites all the unkempt and uncouth hippie Jesus freaks into their prim and proper church, and the deacons pitch a fit and start to leave.

In a poignant scene around this point in the movie, the drifter-hippie turned preacher, Lonnie Frisbee (ironically played by Jonathan Roumie, who plays the part of Jesus in *The Chosen*), says to Chuck Smith (pastor of Calvary Chapel, played by Kelsey Grammer),

> There is an entire generation out there searching for God. My people are a desperate bunch, and desperation—there is power in that word. What would it take for you, Chuck Smith, to become desperate?[2]

I think I cried for the rest of the movie after that.

Paul is desperate to reach the lost gentiles, but he has to teach the Jews that they aren't in a position to judge. What we are witnessing here is the master stroke of the gospel. Before Jesus lifts, he first levels. All the status markers in the house, especially religious ones, must go. Truth be told, this is what most churches need most. We need the most religious people in the house to rend their hearts and repent. We need the families who think they own the church and run the place to stand down and make room. The gospel is a wrecking ball for comfortable, conventional, respectable religion. The ground is level at the foot of the cross. Why does this matter?

Because there is an entire generation out there searching for God. What would it take for you to become desperate?

---

2. Jon Erwin and Brent McCorkle, directors, *Jesus Revolution* (Santa Monica, CA: Lionsgate, 2023).

The Prayer

Jesus, we belong to you. Yes, Jesus, I belong to you. Jesus, you are the gospel. We confess we have tried to fit you into our program and make you serve our agendas. We like our familiar crowd and our easy beliefs. Would you level the ground under my feet? Search me and show me the ways I have put myself on a higher level than others. Convict me of my secret pride. Holy Spirit, awaken me to the desperation of Jesus, who is searching for those desperately searching for him. Praying in Jesus's name. Amen.

The Questions

Do you have a sense of desperation for Jesus in your life? In the world around us, do you sense the desperation other people feel for Jesus—even if they don't identify it as such?

13 | Romans 3:9–18
Why There Is Only One Prayer

> What shall we conclude then? Do we have any advantage? Not at all! For we have already made the charge that Jews and Gentiles alike are all under the power of sin. As it is written:
>
> "There is no one righteous, not even one;
>   there is no one who understands;
>   there is no one who seeks God.
> All have turned away,
>   they have together become worthless;
> there is no one who does good,
>   not even one."
> "Their throats are open graves;
>   their tongues practice deceit."
> "The poison of vipers is on their lips."

> "Their mouths are full of cursing and bitterness."
> "Their feet are swift to shed blood;
> ruin and misery mark their ways,
> and the way of peace they do not know."
> "There is no fear of God before their eyes."

Consider This

Repeat after me—and aloud so your ears can hear it:

>I am not righteous—not even me.
>>I do not understand.
>>I do not seek God.
>>I have turned away.
>>I have become worthless.
>>I do not do good—not even me.
>>My throat is an open grave.
>>My tongue practices deceit.
>>The poison of vipers is on my lips.
>>My mouth is full of cursing and bitterness.
>>My feet are swift to shed blood.
>>My ways are marked by ruin and misery.
>>I do not know the way of peace.
>>My eyes do not see the fear of God.

I know—many of you had a hard time with that because it isn't where you are now. However, at minimum, it is where you were before you met Jesus. It cannot be overstressed to remember who you once were. Even if you did not do these specific sins, Sin was in you. It commanded you, ruled you, and ruined your life, even if everything on the outside had the touch of a master decorator.

When we say with Paul, "I am not ashamed of the gospel," we're acknowledging who we were. We are saying, This was me, my lot, my reality, even if I didn't fully realize it at the time. I was under the power of capital-S Sin. I could do nothing to free myself.

This is the reason why many decent, God-fearing, church-going people aren't really saved from Sin—because they haven't yet realized they were under the power of Sin, which is another way of saying they still are. To justify oneself by saying, "I am baptized," is just like a Jew in Bible times saying, "I am circumcised." The gospel is not skin level. It is deep heart level. It gets down into your guts where shame hides and tries to convince you it's not there.

It's why at the end of the day I contend there is only one prayer and one prayer alone. And it goes like this:

Lord Jesus Christ, Son of God, have mercy on me, a sinner.

The Prayer

Yes, Jesus, "I am not ashamed of the gospel, because it is the power of God that brings salvation to everyone who believes." I confess that something in me wants to believe Jesus is a great Savior without believing I am a gross sinner. Seeing myself that way offends my pride, which is another way of saying it stokes my shame. So I will say it here before you, Jesus, not as a self-condemning statement but as the liberating words of the honest truth—I am a gross sinner. It was far worse than I realized. And I am now beginning to know you are far greater than I ever could have imagined. Something about knowing who I once was opens me up to knowing who you most truly are and who I am most truly becoming. Yes, Jesus, this is the way. You are the way. Praying in your name. Amen.

The Questions

Are you tracking? Struggling? Does something in you resist confessing—not your sins but your Sin? I am a great sinner. Jesus is a great Savior.

Week 2: Discussion Questions

Hearing the Text
Read Romans 2:5–3:18.

Responding to the Text
- What did you hear?
- What did you see?
- What did you otherwise sense from the Lord?

Sharing Insights and Implications for Discipleship
Drawing from the Scripture text and daily readings, what did you find challenging, encouraging, provocative, comforting, invasive, inspiring, corrective, affirming, guiding, or warning?

Shaping Intentions for Prayer
Write your discipleship intention for the week ahead.

3
WEEK

Romans 3:19–4:12

Romans 3:19–20

15   Jesus Paid It All

> Now we know that whatever the law says, it says to those who are under the law, so that every mouth may be silenced and the whole world held accountable to God. Therefore no one will be declared righteous in God's sight by the works of the law; rather, through the law we become conscious of our sin.

Consider This

Near the end of his life, John Newton, author of the hymn "Amazing Grace," said these words:

> My memory is nearly gone; but I remember two things: that I am a great sinner, and that Christ is a great Saviour.[1]

The purpose of the Law is to make us conscious of our sins. On this point, the Bible is clear.

In other words, the Law wasn't given so people would endlessly strive to fulfill it and consider they were doing a pretty good job. It was given to show us our desperate need of God and our hopelessness to obey it apart from him.

In other words, the Law was given to reveal to us the insolvency of our souls. Yes, we are born into bankruptcy. We didn't ask for it. We didn't earn it. It's not fair. You might say we didn't even deserve it. None of this changes the fact of it. This is what the Bible reveals to us about the nature of human beings. We are born debtors because of the sin of our forebears in the garden. Though we didn't create the original debt, we have added to its immensity.

Here's the problem I have. I have debts, but I don't much think of

---

1. John Pollock, *Amazing Grace: John Newton's Story* (San Francisco: Harper & Row, 1981), 182.

myself as a debtor. And I surely don't think of myself as bankrupt. (Well, maybe a little bit, but that's for another day.) But doesn't that tell the story? There's no such thing as a little bit bankrupt. Our capital-S Sin has put us into the condition known as bankruptcy. Our little-s sins are like the interest adding up on the debt. We can never repay it. It's kind of like the national debt of the United States. As of now, it stands at $36 trillion dollars. Yet somehow all of us are able to walk around and live our lives like it is not even real. We certainly don't own the fact that we have had anything to do with it. Nevertheless, the day is coming when that debt will come due. Though it can be extended and extended, it can't be extinguished unless it is repaid.

It is the same with our sins. We can walk around for a long time carrying a debt we can never repay—just racking up interest—and living our lives like it's not even real. At the same time, it is taking its cruel toll on our souls, bit by bit, day by day. The day is coming when that debt will come due. Whether or not we want to face it, there will be a judgment, an accounting, a calling of the note.

It is a terrible, awful thing (even shameful) to be in so much debt without hope of repaying it. It leads to the searing of the conscience and the hardening of the heart.

It's why the gospel is such a song: "Jesus paid it all. All to him I owe. Sin had left a crimson stain. He washed it white as snow."[2]

Again, what can wash away my sin? Nothing but the blood of Jesus.

Again, "My sin, O the bliss of this glorious thought; my sin not in part but the whole is nailed to the cross and I bear it no more. Praise the Lord, Praise the Lord, oh my soul."[3]

The Prayer

Jesus, I am not ashamed of the gospel for it is the power of God for the salvation of everyone who believes. And I believe. Part of me is ashamed of my bankrupt soul, and yet you came and paid it all. It is too good to be true, and yet it is

---

2. Elvina M. Hall, "Jesus Paid It All," 1865.
3. Horatio Spafford, "It Is Well with My Soul," 1873.

true. I receive it, Jesus, as an unworthy, grateful sinner. I receive it. Praise the Lord, Praise the Lord, oh, my soul. Praying in Jesus's name. Amen.

The Questions

Does the debt and bankruptcy metaphor help you grasp the nature of sin and the grace of salvation? Do you struggle to confess the bankruptcy of your soul—as you once were? How about now?

Romans 3:21–26
16 | The Second Mic Drop in Romans

> But now apart from the law the righteousness of God has been made known, to which the Law and the Prophets testify. This righteousness is given through faith in Jesus Christ to all who believe. There is no difference between Jew and Gentile, for all have sinned and fall short of the glory of God, and all are justified freely by his grace through the redemption that came by Christ Jesus. God presented Christ as a sacrifice of atonement, through the shedding of his blood—to be received by faith. He did this to demonstrate his righteousness, because in his forbearance he had left the sins committed beforehand unpunished—he did it to demonstrate his righteousness at the present time, so as to be just and the one who justifies those who have faith in Jesus.

Consider This

Today, dear ones, we have witnessed what is referred to as a mic drop.

My dear friends in Jesus, we have heard the gospel today as handwritten by Saul of Tarsus, *the* apostle Paul, somewhere around the year of our Lord 50. There's a lot to be said about what Paul said, but I am moved to simply slow-walk us through what the Holy Spirit is saying here. We need to savor it, relish it, treasure it in our hearts, and ponder it. I'm going to insert line breaks like it's a poem, like the divine verse that it is:

> But now
> apart from the law
> the righteousness of God
> has been made known,
> to which the Law and the Prophets testify.
> This righteousness is given
> through faith in Jesus Christ
> to all who believe.
> There is no difference between Jew and Gentile,
> for all have sinned
> and fall short
> of the glory of God,
> and all are justified freely
> by his grace
> through the redemption
> that came by Christ Jesus.
> God presented Christ as a sacrifice of atonement,
> through the shedding of his blood—
> to be received
> by faith.
> He did this to demonstrate his righteousness,
> because in his forbearance
> he had left the sins committed beforehand
> unpunished—
> he did it to demonstrate his righteousness
> at the present time,
> so as to be just and
> the one who justifies those
> who have faith in Jesus.

[Full stop.]
Mic drop.

The Prayer

Jesus, we belong to you, and we are not ashamed of the gospel for it is the power of God for the salvation of everyone who believes—and for me. Thank you that your Word is powerful, full of grace and truth, and mighty to save. I hear these words, Jesus, but there are places in my heart and mind needing to hear them deeper. Holy Spirit, search me and find those hard places, those resistant places where I am not moved by this good news. Awaken me to more of you. Only then will I be less of the me I used to be and more of the me I was made to be. Praying in Jesus's name. Amen.

The Questions

How does the biblical text today move you? Does it impact you as much as you would like it to? Do you feel in some ways you have been inoculated from the gospel (i.e., gotten just enough of it to keep you from really getting it)?

Romans 3:27–31

17 | Has Anyone Ever Paid Your Debts?

> *Where, then, is boasting? It is excluded. Because of what law? The law that requires works? No, because of the law that requires faith. For we maintain that a person is justified by faith apart from the works of the law. Or is God the God of Jews only? Is he not the God of Gentiles too? Yes, of Gentiles too, since there is only one God, who will justify the circumcised by faith and the uncircumcised through that same faith. Do we, then, nullify the law by this faith? Not at all! Rather, we uphold the law.*

Consider This

Most everyone understands what it means to carry debt and the onerous burden it can impose over time. Many people work very long and diligently to pay off all their debts, and when they get to the last penny it is an occasion of exuberant celebration. It evokes an appropriate kind of pride-filled boasting in them to be debt free. It is the kind of thing you want others to know about and celebrate with you.

There is a similar sense of pride in legalistic types of religious people about their hard-fought rule-keeping righteousness. They want others to know, and they find ways of letting their righteous deeds be known. There are brazen ways of wearing one's religion on one's sleeve, and then there are quite sophisticated ways of doing so. Jesus hates this. He loves the humility of hidden righteousness and the quiet deeds of secret goodness.

In our recent history my family endured a ten-year train wreck of tragedy. One of the outcomes of this season was the accrual of significant debts I could not repay. I referenced in a prior entry that I might know a little something about the brink of bankruptcy. One early morning in those days, Bill and Phyllis Johnson heard Jesus call them to "pay J. D. Walt's debts." Not knowing the amount or extent, they contacted me and shared their intention. Later that day they did it. I can't begin to tell you the enormous blessing and gift this was to me—to all of a sudden become free of multiple debts that it would have taken decades to repay—especially in the face of the reality that I would soon be responsible for four children in college at the same time. It was one of the signal "God moments" in my life for which I will be eternally grateful. Beyond the money, it represented to me something well past what words can convey—the extravagant love of God.

I love what Paul says in today's text—*Where, then, is boasting?*

This is the moment when you begin to boast in Jesus. Now imagine having the unpayable debt of your soul paid in full by Jesus, by his atoning blood. It is not only the retirement of the capital-S Sin debt but the reversal of bankruptcy and all its penalties and ruinous consequences. It means the restoration of your full faith and credit. It means being made better than whole. No matter how bad the present-day and future consequences of our inherited debt of Sin and all the debts and interest we have personally added, how good and even greater are the consequences of the saving grace of Jesus Christ. And as we will see through the unfolding letter to the Romans, it is not a mere future benefit to be received at our death. It is an overwhelming gift of abundant life beginning immediately.

Few things are more surprising and joyful than when someone comes in and pays your debts with no expectation of being paid back. This is what Jesus has done for us beyond belief. That's why it requires faith to realize the truth of this gift. This is what it means to be saved by grace through faith. Faith is not assenting to the truth of something arguably real. No, faith is the complete reliance on the reality of something demonstratively true. Faith does not mean, "I believe in Jesus." Faith means, "I belong to Jesus."

The Prayer

Jesus, we belong to you. Yes, Jesus, I belong to you. These are not the mere words of my mouth. They are not merely the hope of my aspiration. No, these words are the bedrock truth of my reality. I belong to you, and you belong to me. This is my life. You are my life. I welcome the fullness of your durable reality right here and right now. Thank you for paying my debt in full. Thank you that your credit is now my credit. Holy Spirit, please awaken me to fully realize these eternal verities as realities on which I stake everything. Praying in Jesus's name. Amen.

The Questions

Are you waking up to more of what Jesus has done and is doing for, in, and through you and your life? Are you at least waking up to your need and longing to awaken more to these eternal verities that they may become present-day lived realities for you?

Romans 4:1-3

18 | Faith: From Beliefs to Believing

> What then shall we say that Abraham, our forefather according to the flesh, discovered in this matter? If, in fact, Abraham was justified by works, he had something to boast about—but not before God. What does Scripture say? "Abraham believed God, and it was credited to him as righteousness."

=== **Consider This** ===

Let's reach back to that first mic drop in Romans 1.

> For I am not ashamed of the gospel, because it is the power of God that brings salvation to everyone who believes: first to the Jew, then to the Gentile. For in the gospel the righteousness of God is revealed—a righteousness that is by faith from first to last, just as it is written: "The righteous will live by faith." (Rom. 1:16–17)

So far we have learned about a so-called righteousness that comes by striving and struggling and trying to justify yourself by good behavior and through following the rules. This would be the way of self-reliance that leads to self-righteousness. And though we are no longer Jews trying to keep the Mosaic Law, this impulse and mode of operation is alive and well in human beings to the present day. Self-righteousness that comes from self-reliance moving toward self-justification is not righteousness at all; rather, it is a form of slavery. In fact, it is a counterfeit righteousness.

Paul contrasts this with the gospel of Jesus Christ, which is about a righteousness that is being revealed from heaven. This is not a righteousness that can be worked for or somehow achieved or earned. It is a gift that comes by grace through faith. It can only be received. The fact that it is being "revealed" means we never could have figured it out, much less invented it ourselves.

And what is this righteousness? It is the deep longing of our hearts for the deep rightness of true goodness. I would say it is the holy fire that burns at the intersection of justice and mercy and of forgiveness and peace and of love and faith. Admittedly, these are idealistic abstract values until they all show up in perfect union in the same person, the Holy One of God—Jesus of Nazareth, the Messiah.

Jesus Christ is the revelation of the righteousness of God, and in receiving him through faith—his life, death, resurrection, and ascension—our lives become restored, redeemed, and refashioned to live faithfully as the image bearers of God for our good, others' gain, and God's glory.

The word *faithful* sounds like effort, but it actually means something more like the energy of God, as in faith-full. We aren't filled with our own faith but by the faith of the indwelling presence of Jesus Christ himself. It is why Scripture will later call him both the pioneer and perfecter of our faith (Hebrews 12:2).

Faith is not something we are trying to do well or to somehow get right. It is rather an immersive participation in the very life of God—on earth as it is in heaven. To be full of faith is to be infused by the life of God in such a way that crucifies our old sin-sick life and reveals our resurrected life in Jesus Christ, filled by the Holy Spirit to live the glorious life human beings were originally intended to live. All along, from the first day to the present day, from first to last, we were intended to live by faith.

> What does Scripture say? "Abraham believed God, and it was credited to him as righteousness."

Part of our problem comes in the way we interchangeably use the terms *believe* and *faith*. We quickly move from the word *believe* to *beliefs*, and faith morphs from the risk of believing God to the relative safety of our "beliefs" about God. Notice the text does not say Abraham believed in God. It says Abraham believed God—which is to say he staked his very life and future on God.

The Prayer

Jesus, we belong to you. Yes, Jesus, I belong to you. Thank you for the gospel, through which you reveal to us—in your life, death, resurrection, ascension, and reign—a righteousness that is from first to last by faith. Give us this faith that we might receive this gift of grace and so live into and out of this righteousness. Holy Spirit, shift us from believing in things about God to actually believing God. Praying in Jesus's name. Amen.

The Questions

How would you define and describe what faith is? Is it a belief, or is it believing? And how do you see the difference?

Romans 4:4–8

19

The Difference Between Knowing What We Believe and Knowing Who We Believe

> *Now to the one who works, wages are not credited as a gift but as an obligation. However, to the one who does not work but trusts God who justifies the ungodly, their faith is credited as righteousness. David says the same thing when he speaks of the blessedness of the one to whom God credits righteousness apart from works:*
>
> *"Blessed are those*
>   *whose transgressions are forgiven,*
>   *whose sins are covered.*
> *Blessed is the one*
>   *whose sin the Lord will never count against them."*

===== **Consider This** =====

I am trying to wrap my mind around the gospel—the power of God for the salvation of all who believe.

It is like I am getting credit for something I did not do or earn.

It is like I failed an exam. But someone retook the exam for me and got 100 percent, and I was awarded that grade and passed the class. I was declared graduated.

It is like I committed a crime and was in jail awaiting trial. Someone bailed me out of jail; only they went to jail in my place. Then they stood trial for my crime and pleaded guilty even though they weren't guilty. Then served the prison sentence. And all of that counted for me. I was fully pardoned.

It is like I was in debt beyond my ability to ever pay it back. Someone paid all my debts, telling me I not only didn't have to pay the debts but I didn't have to pay the person back either. I was declared debt free.

We tend to view each of these kinds of scenarios as situations we either found our way into because of our own failures or avoided because of our own successes. The message of the gospel says no such thing. The gospel reveals these scenarios as the very realities into which we were born. We are born under and into the power of Sin. Salvation is about being reborn under and into the power of grace.

These are the terms of the gospel. Have you or are you reckoning with the terms of the gospel? Are they like the terms of a software agreement on your computer or phone that you quickly scroll through without attention and click "accept" at the end? Or are you grappling with these terms as the mind-bending realities of the goodness of God?

Everything in me feels an enormous relief and extraordinary gratitude for being delivered from such impossible and dooming scenarios and given complete freedom—fresh life and a new start. I feel embraced.

At the same time, there is something in me that looks down on myself for being such a poor wretched soul in the first place. I want to think better of myself. I want to believe I had or have what it takes to do this on my own and by my own means and wherewithal. And further, I want to believe I can take it all from here and manage just fine without further aid. Why? Because I also feel embarrassed.

So many of us have "believed" the terms of the gospel as mere "beliefs" and "accepted" Jesus as our Savior as though salvation merely required mental assent. I am not here questioning or calling into question the veracity of what happened in your past. I am merely asking you to grapple with it at a much deeper level. I am asking you to invite Jesus, through the Holy Spirit, to first ransack and then renovate your mind by the terms of his gospel. We have to press past the "what" of our beliefs and deep into the "who" of whom we believe.

I love how the old gospel hymn puts it: "But I know whom I have believed, and am persuaded that He is able to keep that which I've committed unto Him against that day."[4]

I am concerned that much of the church and many of us who bear the name Christian have bought into a truncated and superficial version of the gospel of Jesus Christ that is not really the gospel at all. I believe this is the very kind of thing Paul was saying to the Jews of his time concerning their faith and religion. It's why he goes all the way back to Abraham. He's stripping things back, even bare. He's going back to first things. That's what I'm asking us to do.

The Prayer

Jesus, I belong to you. And yet I ask you, "Do I really?" I invite you to turn on the searchlight of your Spirit in the halls and chambers of my heart. I give you permission to ransack the thin religion I may have created there, even unwittingly. I am weary of carrying around a self-assuredness that is not the assurance of the Spirit. I am tired of professing a salvation that is hardly skin deep. I want the real gospel, the deep truth, the renovating righteousness that comes by faith as a gift—the credit I did not earn—and that embarrasses and embraces me at the same time. Yes, Holy Spirit, more of this. Praying in Jesus's name. Amen.

The Questions

Do you have a sense that we (even you) may have adopted a truncated and superficial version of the gospel of Jesus Christ? How so? Are you

---

4. Daniel W. Whittle, "I Know Not Why God's Wonderous Grace," 1883.

willing to have this revealed to you? And to reach deeper? And deepening doesn't mean discounting what has gone before. God wastes nothing.

20

Romans 4:9–12

The Man on the Middle Cross Said I Could Come

> Is this blessedness only for the circumcised, or also for the uncircumcised? We have been saying that Abraham's faith was credited to him as righteousness. Under what circumstances was it credited? Was it after he was circumcised, or before? It was not after, but before! And he received circumcision as a sign, a seal of the righteousness that he had by faith while he was still uncircumcised. So then, he is the father of all who believe but have not been circumcised, in order that righteousness might be credited to them. And he is then also the father of the circumcised who not only are circumcised but who also follow in the footsteps of the faith that our father Abraham had before he was circumcised.

=== **Consider This** ===

What do Abraham and circumcision have to do with today's text? The eleven most powerful words in the fourth chapter of Romans, if not in the whole letter, and maybe the whole Bible (there I go again) are these:

> Abraham believed God, and it was credited to him as righteousness.

Circumcision is not required. The Law is not required. Good works are not required. So far so good. Let's take it a step further. The sinner's prayer is not required. Baptism is not required. Going to church is not required. The only thing required: believing God.

Truth #1: We bring nothing. Truth #2: God brings everything. And when we can finally wrap our minds around truth #1 and #2, then we will have something. It is through that something we become the kind of people through whom God can do anything.

So what is that something? It is faith. It is not believing in God, or believing in a set of doctrines about God—true as they may be—but believing God.

Alistair Begg, senior pastor of Cleveland's Parkside Church, preached a rousing sermon on the thief on the cross. He remembered the interchange between the two thieves on either side of Jesus at Calvary. Then he recalled the one thief's plea to Jesus: "Remember me when you come into your kingdom" and Jesus's merciful response: "Today you will be with me in paradise." Begg imagines the wild interchange in heaven when the thief arrives:

> Think about the thief on the cross. . . . I can't wait to find that fellow one day to ask him, "How did that shake out for you? Because you were cussing the guy out with your friend. You'd never been in a Bible study. You'd never got baptized. You didn't know a thing about church membership. And yet—and yet, you made it! You made it! How did you make it?"
>
> That's what the angel must have said—you know, like, "What are you doing here?"
>
> "Well, I don't know."
>
> "What do you mean, you don't know?"
>
> "Well, 'cause I don't know."
>
> "Well, you know . . . excuse me. Let me get my supervisor."
>
> They go get the supervisor angel: "So, we've just a few questions for you. First of all, are you clear on the doctrine of justification by faith?"
>
> The guy says, "I've never heard of it in my life."
>
> "And what about . . . Let's just go to the doctrine of Scripture immediately."
>
> This guy's just staring.
>
> And eventually, in frustration, he says, "On what basis are you here?"
>
> And he said, "The man on the middle cross said I could come."

Now, that is the only answer. That is the only answer. And if I don't preach the gospel to myself all day and every day, then I will find myself beginning to trust myself and trust my experience, which is part of my fallenness as a man. If I take my eyes off the cross, I can then give only lip service to its efficacy while at the same time living as if my salvation depends upon me. And as soon as you go there, it will lead you either to abject despair or a horrible kind of arrogance. And it is only the cross of Christ that deals both with the dreadful depths of despair and the pretentious arrogance of the pride of man that says, "You know, I can figure this out, and I'm doing wonderfully well." No.

> Because the sinless Savior died,
> My sinful soul is counted free;
> For God the just is satisfied
> To look on Him and pardon me.[5]

The man on the middle cross said I could come.

The Prayer

Abba Father, Lord Jesus Christ, Blessed Holy Spirit, have mercy on us sinners. We pray with Charles Wesley, "Depth of mercy! Can there be mercy still reserved for me? Can my God His wrath forbear? Me, the chief of sinners, spare?"[6] We confess we bring nothing to the cross, while you bring everything. Today, we—no, I—receive your everything in exchange for my nothing. I receive the gift of your grace by my wholehearted faith. Indeed, we say with the thief, "The man on the middle cross said I could come." Thank you for receiving my faith and crediting it to me as righteousness.

---

5. Alistair Begg, "The Man on the Middle Cross Said I Can Come | Alistair Begg," YouTube, June 17, 2021, https://www.youtube.com/watch?v=xk9wgJBoEd8&t=232s; last stanza is Begg quoting Charitie L. Bancroft, "Before the Throne of God Above," 1863.
6. Charles Wesley, "Depth of Mercy," 1872.

The Questions

Do you struggle with adding requirements to the grace of God—for yourself, for others? Why? Is it enough that the man on the middle cross said you could come? Do you believe God?

Week 3: Discussion Questions

Hearing the Text

Read Romans 3:19–4:12.

Responding to the Text

- What did you hear?
- What did you see?
- What did you otherwise sense from the Lord?

Sharing Insights and Implications for Discipleship

Drawing from the Scripture text and daily readings, what did you find challenging, encouraging, provocative, comforting, invasive, inspiring, corrective, affirming, guiding, or warning?

Shaping Intentions for Prayer

Write your discipleship intention for the week ahead.

Week 3:
Discussion Questions

Hearing the Text
Read Romans 12:1-13.

Responding to the Text
- What did you hear?
- What, if anything, surprised you?
- What did you hear or sense anew from the Lord?

Sharing Insights and Implications for Discipleship
Describe insights, discoveries, and daily leading you are discerning that are challenging, encouraging, or penetrating/conforming to you or inspiring repentance, affirming, and/or new life.

Shaping Intentions for Prayer
Write your discipleship intention for the week ahead.

WEEK 4

Romans 4:13–5:17

Romans 4:13–17

22 | Back to the Second Beginning . . .

> It was not through the law that Abraham and his offspring received the promise that he would be heir of the world, but through the righteousness that comes by faith. For if those who depend on the law are heirs, faith means nothing and the promise is worthless, because the law brings wrath. And where there is no law there is no transgression.
>
> Therefore, the promise comes by faith, so that it may be by grace and may be guaranteed to all Abraham's offspring—not only to those who are of the law but also to those who have the faith of Abraham. He is the father of us all. As it is written: "I have made you a father of many nations." He is our father in the sight of God, in whom he believed—the God who gives life to the dead and calls into being things that were not.

Consider This

We have said a fair amount about Abraham. It would be fitting to remember how this all began. Adam and Eve did not believe God, resulting in the catastrophic collapse of the human race into the sloven shame of sin. So God chose another couple, Abraham and Sarah.

The LORD had said to Abram, "Go from your country, your people and your father's household to the land I will show you.

> "I will make you into a great nation,
>   and I will bless you;
> I will make your name great,
>   and you will be a blessing.
> I will bless those who bless you,
>   and whoever curses you I will curse;
> and all peoples on earth
>   will be blessed through you."

So Abram went, as the LORD had told him; and Lot went with him. Abram was seventy-five years old when he set out from Harran. (Gen. 12:1–4)

In the beginning, God began with a couple who perfectly embodied and expressed the image of God. They became deceived and confused, which led to betrayal and disobedience. Not so this time. God chose a couple who had nothing going for them. For starters, he chose two from among the fallen. And did I mention they were advanced in years? This wouldn't have been such a problem had God not willed to launch a nation. Yes, he willed to start a nation, a people, even a kingdom through their lineage—and yet they were childless. Not only were they childless, but

> without weakening in his faith, [Abraham] faced the fact that his body was as good as dead—since he was about a hundred years old—and that Sarah's womb was also dead.

In other words, they had no potential. Nevertheless, God picked them to lead. They were the perfect exemplars of the law of sin and death. They were dead in their sin, dead in their bodies, dead in their hopes—dead in every way dead could be dead, except they had a pulse.

This is who God chooses to awaken the world from the law of sin and death to the way of faith and righteousness. It's why today's text adds this bit at the end—*the God who gives life to the dead and calls into being things that were not.*

I have tended to think of salvation in legal terms for a lot of my life, even transactional. We believe in Jesus and his work on our behalf, and it is credited to us as righteousness. End of story. Now Paul has me thinking quite differently. It's more like Abraham looking into the night sky and hearing the voice of God telling him his descendants would be more numerous than all the starry host—and Abraham believing him even though he remained childless.

What if we are missing the point when it comes to salvation by grace through faith? What if it is vastly larger than a cosmic (albeit legal) transaction—way more than a mere pardon? What if it is about resurrection from the dead—even before you die—and the appropriation of eternal life even before eternity begins? After all, you saw the text. We are dealing with

> the God who gives life to the dead and calls into being things that were not.

The Prayer

Jesus, I belong to you. What if that's my act of faith, to live as though that were the truest thing in the universe? This is far more than a forensic transaction. This is a catastrophic transformation. Indeed, "long my imprisoned spirit lay fast-bound in sin and nature's night. Thine eye diffused a quickening ray. I woke the dungeon flamed with light. My chains fell off. My heart was free. I rose, went forth, and followed Thee."[1] Thank you for teaching me to believe you with everything I've got. Praying in Jesus's name. Amen.

The Questions

Could it be that we have focused so much on sin and salvation that we have lost the bigger story of salvation—of being swept up into the very death and resurrection of Jesus in order to live life in his kingdom, on earth as it is in heaven?

---

23 | Romans 4:18–25
A Wretch like Me?

> Against all hope, Abraham in hope believed and so became the father of many nations, just as it had been said to him, "So shall your offspring be." Without weakening in his faith, he faced the fact that his body was as good as dead—since he was about a hundred years

---

1. Charles Wesley, "And Can It Be That I Should Gain," 1738.

> old—and that Sarah's womb was also dead. Yet he did not waver through unbelief regarding the promise of God, but was strengthened in his faith and gave glory to God, being fully persuaded that God had power to do what he had promised. This is why "it was credited to him as righteousness." The words "it was credited to him" were written not for him alone, but also for us, to whom God will credit righteousness—for us who believe in him who raised Jesus our Lord from the dead. He was delivered over to death for our sins and was raised to life for our justification.

Consider This

> Amazing grace how sweet the sound that saved a
> wretch like me.

Not long ago, as I drove to church on a Sunday, Chris Tomlin came on the radio singing "Amazing Grace." Interestingly, at church one of the pastors, Doc Holiday, sang "Amazing Grace" as an anthem during Communion. Did you know it's the most popular hymn ever written about Jesus that never mentions his name? But I digress. Here's my point:

> Amazing grace how sweet the sound that saved a
> wretch like me.

I'm comfortable with saying, "a wretch like you," but me? Though I always sang it, I'm not sure I ever really meant it . . . until now.

And no, it isn't because I recently did something really bad or wretched.

It is because I am in the midst of having my mind renewed by the truth of God's Word. You know how you can know something but not really know it yet? That's what's happening with me. I'm knowing something I've known before but at a much deeper level.

I thought of the problem with the world and the human race to be one of bad or sinful behavior. And to be sure, this is the presenting problem. But the problem is that the presenting problem is only symptomatic of the much bigger problem. (Okay, read that one again.) I promise I'm not talking in circles. I am and have been well familiar with the symptoms, and yet I have lived in a kind of denial of the real and much deeper sickness. The symptoms seem to destroy us from the outside in. The sickness, however, decimates us from the inside out. While it may present itself in all sorts of devastating outward symptoms, it may just as well be silently destroying us without any external symptoms at all—not so much as a fever.

I am not a wretch because of my behavior, though my behavior to a greater or lesser degree might indicate such. I am a wretch because of my diabolically corrupted nature as a fallen human being. This is why the cross of Jesus Christ cuts to the core issue—my Sinful nature. The cross is not a topical ointment meant to deal only with the forgiveness of my little-s sins. The cross is an arrow from heaven shot through the heart of the sin-sick human race, crucifying sin's power, literally burying us in the grave, resurrecting us in power, and restoring our glory. And all of this is perfectly embodied in and imparted through the life, death, resurrection, and ascension of Jesus Messiah, Savior of the world, Lord of heaven and earth.

> Amazing grace how sweet the sound that saved a wretch like me.

As long as we assess our wretchedness according to our symptomatic behavior, we will miss the crux of the matter and fail to appropriate salvation by grace through faith. Our wretchedness is the very condition of our corrupted human nature and consequently the launchpad of amazing grace. This is not a matter of feeling but of fact.

Can you reckon with the fact? Do you own the fact? Will you accept the diagnosis? Until we do, there will be no cure, only the attempted management of the symptoms, the futile cycle of repeated failure and rededicated effort. Until we face the fact of our hopeless condition, we don't know grace as amazing—only as optimism.

One final bit in this already lengthy entry. Many push back and say, "All that you are saying is not who I am now but who I used to be. As a saved follower of Jesus Christ, I cannot continue to claim the label of sinner and wretch and so forth." Note, the song does not say, "that saved a wretch like I used to be." I find many who equally refuse the other term by which Scripture identifies us: saint. We don't want to claim sainthood for we don't think we are there yet.

Herein lies the dilemma of our stickiness. We don't want to own a former condition or a future one. All the while grace encompasses, infuses, and transforms it all. To the extent I can own who I used to be, I can also own who I am coming to be. Right here and right now, I am sinner and saint, dust and breath, dead to sin and alive to God in Christ.

That's where this train is headed. Romans 5 to 8 hold some of the richest and most revolutionary revelations in all of Scripture. Buckle up.

The Prayer

Yes, Father, my chains are gone. I've been set free. This is amazing grace. Awaken me to the depths of Sin that I may be awakened to the even deeper depths of grace. I am ready for salvation to deepen in me, to press into the width, breadth, height, and length of the love of Jesus Christ. Teach me the mystery of being a sinner and a saint, of remembering who I used to be in such a way that I am freed to run in the path of who I am becoming. Yes, amazing grace, how sweet the sound that saved a wretch like me—even me. Praying in Jesus's name. Amen.

The Questions

Do you struggle to understand and own the nature of your own wretchedness as a sinner who is saved and being saved by grace? Are you grasping better how this is not about bad behavior as much as it is about a corrupted nature?

Romans 5:1–6

24 | How Does Gravity Work?

> *Therefore, since we have been justified through faith, we have peace with God through our Lord Jesus Christ, through whom we have*

> gained access by faith into this grace in which we now stand. And we boast in the hope of the glory of God. Not only so, but we also glory in our sufferings, because we know that suffering produces perseverance; perseverance, character; and character, hope. And hope does not put us to shame, because God's love has been poured out into our hearts through the Holy Spirit, who has been given to us.
>
> You see, at just the right time, when we were still powerless, Christ died for the ungodly.

Consider This

Gravity. Let's try to put our heads around how gravity works.

Physics defines gravity as a force that attracts a body toward the center of the earth, or toward any other physical body having mass.

As a thought exercise, consider two opposing gravitational powers: The power of Sin, which pulls us down into the realm of death, and the power of grace, which pulls us up into the realm of life. This is a helpful framework for me to think through chapters 5 through 8 of Romans.

Before we proceed, let's make clear that these two gravitational powers are in no way equal, as grace is infinitely more powerful than Sin. However, let's also acknowledge that both gravitational powers exert force on our lives at the same time, creating a dire conflicted-ness in the church in the midst of the desperate chaos in the world outside the church. For simplicity's sake, I like to think of them as the gravity of heaven and the gravity of hell.

> Therefore, since we have been justified through faith, we have peace with God through our Lord Jesus Christ, through whom we have gained access by faith into this grace in which we now stand.

As has been noted and yet cannot be overstressed, we are born into the power of Sin and bound in the realm of death (i.e., the gravity of hell). By the mercy of God through the cross of Jesus Christ—in his life, death, resurrection, and ascension—the power of Sin has been broken and the curse of death has been defeated. In other words, human beings can escape the gravity of sin, death, and hell but only by the power of grace and be caught up in the gravity of life and love, which is the realm of heaven.

Now here is the grace of God in its most potent biblical sound bite:

> You see, at just the right time, when we were still powerless, Christ died for the ungodly.

So how does gravity work? It just works. Salvation shifts the center of gravity from the power of Sin to the power of God.

> Therefore, since we have been justified through faith, we have peace with God through our Lord Jesus Christ, through whom we have gained access by faith into this grace in which we now stand.

Faith is not a matter of mere belief in this as true. It is a movement of trust.

The secret is Jesus. He is our center of gravity. He sits at the right hand of God in the heavens—and simultaneously he sits on the throne of our hearts. In other words, amazing grace is the very real life-on-earth-as-it-is-in-heaven. A trusting faith in Jesus is the key, not a passive belief in God.

How does the gravity of the gospel work? Let's give Paul the last word today:

> because God's love has been poured out into our hearts through the Holy Spirit, who has been given to us.

The Prayer

God our Father, thank you for the gospel, who is Jesus Christ, through whom we are delivered from the gravity of Sin, death, and hell and into the gravity of grace, life, and heaven. Thank you that these are not abstract concepts but that they have been fleshed out in the literal physical body of Jesus Christ himself. Holy Spirit, please interpret these things into my deepest mind and heart such that they would flow out and into every fiber of my being and aspect of my everyday life. Jesus, you are the secret. You are the gospel. I belong to you. Praying in your name. Amen.

The Questions

Does the gravity analogy help you to better grasp how both Sin and grace work upon and within our lives? What might it mean for you to walk in faith—to step out of the gravity of Sin and into the gravity of grace?

25 Romans 5:7-8
The Word of the Day and of Eternity

> Very rarely will anyone die for a righteous person, though for a good person someone might possibly dare to die. But God demonstrates his own love for us in this: While we were still sinners, Christ died for us.

Consider This

We have heard a lot of big words in Romans so far. Today, we introduce a new word. We have discussed the weighty concepts of sin and righteousness and faith and justification and mercy and peace and hope and circumcision and the heart and justice and judgment and law and atonement and repentance, and all of this is the stuff of the gospel. Bring all these words together into the deep coherence of the gospel and you get *grace*. But that is not the new word.

As I look over the list of terms, it occurs to me that they are somewhat abstract concepts. They all mean something, and yet their meanings all together point beyond themselves. In other words, they describe something larger. Even this word bringing coherence to them all—*grace*—points beyond itself. They are all nice words, even powerful words with strong meanings, and yet they remain abstractions—until we read this:

> But God demonstrates his own love for us in this: While we were still sinners, Christ died for us.

Amazing grace can only come from one place: amazing love.

As our fight song has it, "He left his Father's throne above, so free so infinite his grace, emptied Himself of all but love, and bled for Adam's helpless race."[2]

The new word is *love*. Though we have hardly seen it to date, we will begin to see it everywhere as we continue in Romans.

Paul refers to the gospel as the "power of God" precisely because the gospel is the love of God. It is why I maintain that rather than the conventional nomenclature of "the gospel of Jesus Christ," it should read, "The gospel is Jesus Christ."

> But God demonstrates his own love for us in this: While we were still sinners, Christ died for us.

Love is the question and the answer. It is the rule and the reason. The love of God in Jesus Christ is not only the grace that saves us; it is also the very life of God in us that makes us agents of salvation for others. The apostle John captures the logic of love in these words: "This is how we know what love is: Jesus Christ laid down his life for us. And we ought to lay down our lives for our brothers and sisters" (1 John 3:16).

> But God demonstrates his own love for us in this: While we were still sinners, Christ died for us.

Grace is an idea. Love can only be a person. Indeed, grace is the big idea of God, but love is his nature and his name.

Yes, "Amazing love how can it be, that thou my God wouldst die for me."[3]

---

2. Charles Wesley, "And Can It Be, That I Should Gain?," 1738.
3. Charles Wesley, "And Can It Be, That I Should Gain?," 1738.

But God demonstrates his own love for us in this: While we were still sinners, Christ died for us.

The Prayer

Our Father in heaven, thank you for sending your Son to this earth to die for us, even for me. I understand this to the point where I can accept it in my understanding, and yet I hardly grasp it. I want to break free into a new level of understanding—not of grasping for you but of being grasped by you. Something tells me this will come down to my willingness to receive and be loved. Something in me doesn't want it to be about love but about power or justice or sovereignty or something that feels weightier to me. Forgive me for this. I think it begins by being honest, so that is my honesty today. I believe my knowledge about you keeps me at a safe distance. I am ready to trade this in for the real knowing and being known by you. I am ready to personally receive the demonstration of love who is Jesus. Praying in his name. Amen.

The Questions

Do you want the gospel to be about something other than love? Why? Does love feel soft and flimsy to you, or has it come into the category of the eternal weight of glory, of ultimate durability and final substance?

Romans 5:9–11
26 | How Much More?

> *Since we have now been justified by his blood, how much more shall we be saved from God's wrath through him! For if, while we were God's enemies, we were reconciled to him through the death of his Son, how much more, having been reconciled, shall we be saved through his life! Not only is this so, but we also boast in God through our Lord Jesus Christ, through whom we have now received reconciliation.*

Consider This

I grew up around two kinds of churches. They sort of had Jesus in common but not really. One kind of church was all about the life of Jesus. They were geared around the stories of Jesus and Jesus as a teacher and an ethical example to emulate. Sure, they talked about his death, but that wasn't emphasized. The other kind of church was all about the death of Jesus and repenting from our sins and being saved. In these churches, the life of Jesus was pretty much reduced to three days in Jerusalem around a hill called Calvary. One focused on his life, and the other on his death. Though these churches were seemingly about the same person and ostensibly had the same goals, they had very little in common. In hindsight, it occurs to me they were both right and yet both wrong. Frankly, I never felt at home in either tradition.

That's what I have long loved about today's text—it paints the whole picture.

> For if, while we were God's enemies, we were reconciled to him through the death of his Son, how much more, having been reconciled, shall we be saved through his life!

We need the death of Jesus. We need the life of Jesus. The stories of Jesus aren't extraneous to the salvation of Jesus. Nor can the gospel be reduced to a three-day span of time in the history of the world. In my thinking, the gospel is the entire story of Jesus—his eternal preexistence, prophesied expectation, conception, birth, childhood, mysterious signs, baptism, miracles, words, wisdom, suffering, death, burial, resurrection, ascension, rule, return, and glorious eternal reign. Nor can Jesus be reduced or confined to the New Testament. He is the whole story of the whole Bible. Whether by allusion or affirmation, every page points to him.

> For if, while we were God's enemies, we were reconciled to him through the death of his Son, how much more, having been reconciled, shall we be saved through his life!

I love how the NIV translates the sentence in that it asks a question and yet it doesn't end with a question mark but an exclamation point. It's another way of saying Jesus is everything. He is the author of the story and its chief actor. We have been reconciled to God through the death of Jesus. How much more, having been reconciled, shall we be saved through his life? Our mission is to answer that question: How much more? It means his life must become the source and substance of our life. As the life of Jesus becomes the depth of our memory, it will become the breadth of our imagination.

The Prayer

Father, we thank you for your Son, Jesus, as we ponder the question, "How much more, having been reconciled, shall we be saved through his life!" We so readily think of salvation as something that happened in our past. Holy Spirit, open the eyes of our hearts to grasp how it is breaking now like news into our present life. Break the life of Jesus out of the compartment we confine him to. Show us the "how much more" his life is saving us. Praying in Jesus's name. Amen.

The Questions

How would you say what I am trying to get across in today's entry? What kind of church have you been most associated with—a "life of Jesus" church or a "death of Jesus" church? Do you see how we must have both in equal focus?

Romans 5:12–17

27 | There Are Only Two Stories

Therefore, just as sin entered the world through one man, and death through sin, and in this way death came to all people, because all sinned—
  To be sure, sin was in the world before the law was given, but

> sin is not charged against anyone's account where there is no law. Nevertheless, death reigned from the time of Adam to the time of Moses, even over those who did not sin by breaking a command, as did Adam, who is a pattern of the one to come.
>
> But the gift is not like the trespass. For if the many died by the trespass of the one man, how much more did God's grace and the gift that came by the grace of the one man, Jesus Christ, overflow to the many! Nor can the gift of God be compared with the result of one man's sin: The judgment followed one sin and brought condemnation, but the gift followed many trespasses and brought justification. For if, by the trespass of the one man, death reigned through that one man, how much more will those who receive God's abundant provision of grace and of the gift of righteousness reign in life through the one man, Jesus Christ!

Consider This

There are only two stories. The story of Adam and the story of Jesus.
> The story of sin and the story of grace.
> The story of death and the story of life.
> The story of crucifixion and the story of resurrection.
> The story of trespass and the story of forgiveness.
> The story of idolatry and the story of worship.
> The story of brokenness and the story of wholeness.
> The story of lost and the story of found.
> The story of darkness and the story of light.
> The story of ashes and the story of beauty.
> The story of empire and the story of kingdom.
> The story of war and the story of peace.
> The story of despair and the story of joy.
> The story of fear and the story of faith.
> The story of condemnation and the story of embrace.
> The story of slavery and the story of freedom.
> The story of injustice and the story of justice.
> The story of pride and the story of humility.
> The story of indifference and the story of love.
> The story of theft and the story of gift.

There are only two stories. The story of Adam and the story of Jesus. Who in their right mind would choose the story of Adam?

And therein lies the problem. We are the unfortunate inheritors of the mind of Adam. The bad news is we are all born into the story of Adam (and Eve). The good news is we are all invited into the story of Jesus. And the story of Jesus is truly a "how much more" story. There is literally no comparison. So why would anyone ever choose to remain in the story of Adam and not take the invitation to enter into the story of Jesus?

There are many reasons, I suppose, but one should concern us the most. People don't take the invitation because they see people who claim to live in the story of Jesus but who have no intention of leaving the story of Adam.

That's not who we are. We are Jesus people. His story is our story. His life is our life. His love is our love. The Holy Spirit is making this a reality for all who accept the invitation and receive the gift. Indeed, the love of God is being poured out into our hearts by the Holy Spirit even now. That's our story. That's our song.

The Prayer

Father, how we thank you for the story of Jesus, who has won, is winning, and will win the battle. What a beautiful story you have held out before us. What a gracious invitation you have delivered to our door. What a compelling life you offer us day after day after day. Forgive us for vacillating between these two ways. Forgive us for remaining of two minds. We confess that our hearts become so easily divided. We need Jesus to heal us before we can wholeheartedly follow him. And that's the miracle, isn't it? While we were still sinners he died for us, making the way open. Holy Spirit, let faith arise in us—deep, defining faith moving in love. Praying in Jesus's name. Amen.

The Questions

Can you add to the litany of our story in today's reading? Are you tired of vacillating between two stories? Between Adam and Jesus? Has your holy discontent reached the tipping point where you are ready to cross over completely?

Week 4: Discussion Questions

Hearing the Text
Read Romans 4:13–5:17.

Responding to the Text
- What did you hear?
- What did you see?
- What did you otherwise sense from the Lord?

Sharing Insights and Implications for Discipleship
Drawing from the Scripture text and daily readings, what did you find challenging, encouraging, provocative, comforting, invasive, inspiring, corrective, affirming, guiding, or warning?

Shaping Intentions for Prayer
Write your discipleship intention for the week ahead.

5
WEEK

Romans 5:18–6:23

Romans 5:18-21

29 — The Soundtrack of the Gospel

> Consequently, just as one trespass resulted in condemnation for all people, so also one righteous act resulted in justification and life for all people. For just as through the disobedience of the one man the many were made sinners, so also through the obedience of the one man the many will be made righteous.
> The law was brought in so that the trespass might increase. But where sin increased, grace increased all the more, so that, just as sin reigned in death, so also grace might reign through righteousness to bring eternal life through Jesus Christ our Lord.

Consider This

Have you learned the soundtrack of the gospel? Paul wrote it down in his letter to the church at Philippi. I'm almost sure the Romans would have seen that letter too and probably sang the song. Imagine Romans 5 as a sermon and Philippians 2:5–11 as the closing hymn. It is the gospel's soundtrack. Now personalize it: Romans 5 is *our* story and Philippians 2 is *our* song.

This song is the perfect setup for Romans 6, which we will dive into next week. Here it is.

Let the same mind be in you that was in Christ Jesus,

>   who, though he existed in the form of God,
>   did not regard equality with God
>   as something to be grasped,
>   but emptied himself,
>   taking the form of a slave,
>   assuming human likeness.
>   And being found in appearance as a human,
>   he humbled himself

> and became obedient to the point of death—
> even death on a cross.
>
> Therefore God exalted him even more highly
> and gave him the name
> that is above every other name,
> so that at the name given to Jesus
> every knee should bend,
> in heaven and on earth and under the earth,
> and every tongue should confess
> that Jesus Christ is Lord,
> to the glory of God the Father. (Philippians 2:5–11 NRSVue)

This hymn is a response to the broken story of Adam. If you trace the story of the hymn, you will see it unfolds in the form of a V, following the journey of Jesus from heaven to earth, all the way down to the cross and the grave and then all the way back up through the resurrection to the ascension and to the final coming of the kingdom.

Now notice something about the story of Adam. It unfolds the opposite journey. It is an ∧ form. The glory of the gospel, who is Jesus Christ, is the way he reverses our course and leads us from the broken story of Adam, depicted in the ∧ form, and into the grand story of grace, depicted in the V form. Prepare now for your mind to be blown by how this plays out:

> ∧ Adam (Eve) was created in the very image of God and yet considered equality with God something to be grasped. "When you eat from it your eyes will be opened, and you will be like God, knowing good and evil" (Genesis 3:5).
> V Jesus was the very image of God himself yet "did not consider equality with God something to be used to his own advantage" (Philippians 2:6).
> ∧ Adam, being a human being bearing God's image, tried to make himself something higher.

V Jesus, the image of God in the form of a human being, made himself nothing and took on the nature of a slave.

∧ Adam became disobedient to the word of God, covered his shame, and then hid in pride from God and thereby introduced sin and death into the created order.

V Jesus humbled himself and became obedient to death, bearing our shame, being exposed in nakedness, not in hiding but in public view.

∧ Adam's rebellion at the Tree of the Knowledge of Good and Evil brought a curse on the entire human race.

V Jesus, by his death on the cross, reversed Adam's rebellion by taking on the curse of Adam. "Cursed is everyone who is hung on a pole" (Galatians 3:13).

∧ Adam and Eve and all their progeny to the present day have fallen to the lowest place.

V Jesus was exalted by the Father to the highest place in his resurrection and ascension.

∧ The curse of Adam continued forward through Cain murdering his brother Abel in the quest for a better name and forward until the entire human community was building a tower to reach the heavens in order to make a great name for themselves.

V Jesus climbed all the way down from the heights of heaven to be crucified on the towering, contemptible cross, and he was *given* the name that is above every name.

∧ Because of the disobedience of Adam, the entire human race is born into a state of rebellion against God.

V Because of the obedience of Jesus's faith, the entire human race (the living and the dead) will ultimately kneel (willingly or otherwise) before the risen and returning Lamb of God and be judged according to the obedience of faith and the righteousness of grace.

∧ Because of the disobedience of Adam and his progeny, the language of the human race was confused and all the people scattered in enmity.

V Because of the obedience of Jesus's faith, every tongue will confess—in an agreement of diverse unity, in all the many distinctive and varied languages of the whole world—the very same affirmation: Jesus Christ is Lord, to the glory of God the Father.

Indeed, the heavenly throngs are already gathering in the midst of angels and archangels, in the presence of the elders and the living beings and the white-robed witnesses from every nation, tribe, and tongue, all circling the throne of God where sits the risen Lord of heaven and earth, the Lamb slain from before the foundation of the world, the King of Kings and the Lord of Lords, Jesus Messiah. And he shall reign forever and ever. Amen.

The Prayer

Today for our prayer, let's remember the words of Hebrews 12:18–24, 28–29:

You have not come to a mountain that can be touched and that is burning with fire; to darkness, gloom and storm; to a trumpet blast or to such a voice speaking words that those who heard it begged that no further word be spoken to them, because they could not bear what was commanded: "If even an animal touches the mountain, it must be stoned to death." The sight was so terrifying that Moses said, "I am trembling with fear."

But you have come to Mount Zion, to the city of the living God, the heavenly Jerusalem. You have come to thousands upon thousands of angels in joyful assembly, to the church of the firstborn, whose names are written in heaven. You have come to God, the Judge of all, to the spirits of the righteous made perfect, to Jesus the mediator of a new covenant, and to the sprinkled blood that speaks a better word than the blood of Abel. . . .

Therefore, since we are receiving a kingdom that cannot be shaken, let us be thankful, and so worship God acceptably with reverence and awe, for our "God is a consuming fire."

Praying in Jesus's name. Amen.

The Questions

My gosh! Some days there are no more questions—only awestruck glory. Today is one of those days.

---

30 Romans 6:1–4
What Jesus Left Behind in the Tomb

> *What shall we say, then? Shall we go on sinning so that grace may increase? By no means! We are those who have died to sin; how can we live in it any longer? Or don't you know that all of us who were baptized into Christ Jesus were baptized into his death? We were therefore buried with him through baptism into death in order that, just as Christ was raised from the dead through the glory of the Father, we too may live a new life.*

Consider This

Two sites around the ancient city of Jerusalem compete for the prize of being the place of the cross and the empty tomb. If you go there, you will undoubtedly visit both sites. The first is known as the Church of the Holy Sepulchre. It is a massive cathedral-like building that meanders across the space of what feels like a small city block. Inside the cathedral is a place that authorities say is *the* spot where Jesus was crucified on the cross. Nearby, also in the cathedral, is the empty tomb. Interestingly, the place feels like neither a cathedral nor an empty tomb. Across town, actually outside the gates of the Old City, is the other site, known as the Garden Tomb. There's a rocky crag on which you can trace the contours of a skull (i.e., Golgotha), and nearby is an ancient cave-like tomb cut into the side of a small hill complete with a large stone next to the mouth of the cave. This has all the "feels" of the place and yet less verification as the authentic site. All this to say, I have been in both empty tombs, and both hold enormous gravitas.

Throughout all the centuries most of the emphasis has been on the fact that the tomb is empty. It's true. The tomb could not hold the risen body of Jesus Christ. He is not there; nor are his bones. In another sense, however, it is not empty. It is quite full. It is filled with the Sin of Adam and all the sins of all the saints from all the ages. As Jesus was crucified on the cross, he took on himself, in his body, the Sin of Adam and the sins of the world past, present, and future. Further, as Jesus's body was laid in the tomb, the Sin of Adam and all the sins of the world, past, present, and future were laid there in his body. We—our Sin and our sins—both crucified and buried Jesus. "They" did not kill Jesus. We did. (And of course "we" includes "them" too.) As Jesus rose from the dead, he left the Sin and the sins in the grave, buried, dead, lifeless, forever.

> Or don't you know that all of us who were baptized into Christ Jesus were baptized into his death? We were therefore buried with him through baptism into death.

Our Sin and our sins are buried in a tomb outside the city gates of what was once Old Jerusalem. They are dead, rotten and ever rotting, dead to us, dead to eternity, forever dead and buried. They have no life, no power, no gravity but that which we accede to them—which is an utter absurdity and only betrays the reality that we have a very inadequate understanding of the death and resurrection of Jesus. This is Paul's point in the opening salvo of Romans 6.

> We are those who have died to sin; how can we live in it any longer?

When Jesus was laid in the tomb, we were laid there with him—our old self, our old life, our Sin, and our sins. When Jesus rose from the dead, we rose with him, our new self, our new life, free from sin and delivered from death.

> We were therefore buried with him through baptism into death

> in order that, just as Christ was raised from the dead through
> the glory of the Father, we too may live a new life.

We have many and varied understandings of what Christian baptism is and what it means. Paul gives us the ground zero definitive picture of it here in Romans 6.

Death. Burial. Resurrection.

Right here and right now.

I fear we have largely missed the point when it comes to baptism. We have majored in the minors while debating over trivialities. Baptism is first and foremost about Jesus's death, Jesus's burial, and Jesus's resurrection. He went to the cross and carried our Sin and our sins. His friends carried his lifeless body, murdered by Sin and sins, and laid him in the tomb. Our Sin and our sins and our old life were buried in the literal tomb in Jerusalem. Jesus was raised from the dead, and as he ran out of that grave, our new life—our delivered-from-death life—and our freedom from sin ran out with him. And we are still running free from sin and full of faith in the newness of life today.

You see, baptism is not a symbolic rite of passage as we are prone to believe. It is a literal living participation in the real, physical, and embodied deliverance of Jesus Christ from sin and death into life and love, which is freedom.

> We were therefore buried with him through baptism into death
> in order that, just as Christ was raised from the dead through
> the glory of the Father, we too may live a new life.

Reflect deeply on this today, because it is going to get a lot deeper tomorrow and the day after that.

The Prayer

Our Father, how we thank you for your Son, Jesus, who took on our Sin and our sins in his physical body. He took them, and us with them, into the tomb. And he rose from the dead and took us with him, leaving our Sin and our sins behind in the grave forever. Holy Spirit, bring our own baptism back before our memory—open the eyes of our hearts to see what really happened there. Bring us into the depths of remembrance such that we understand our baptism beyond what we did before—that we were buried with him into death in order that we might be raised with him into life. Give us the vision to see our Sin and our sins left behind in that tomb in Jerusalem forever. They are dead to us, and we are dead to them. Praying in Jesus's name. Amen.

The Questions

Are you beginning to see baptism from a fresh angle? Are you seeing what actually happened in baptism? Are you ready to rise up into your baptism in a renewed and revivified and empowered fashion? You are dead to Sin, and Sin is dead to you.

31 Romans 6:5–10
The Day It Started Changing for Me

> For if we have been united with him in a death like his, we will certainly also be united with him in a resurrection like his. For we know that our old self was crucified with him so that the body ruled by sin might be done away with, that we should no longer be slaves to sin—because anyone who has died has been set free from sin.
>
> Now if we died with Christ, we believe that we will also live with him. For we know that since Christ was raised from the dead, he cannot die again; death no longer has mastery over him. The death he died, he died to sin once for all; but the life he lives, he lives to God.

Consider This

My life and faith changed quite dramatically in my early twenties. Romans 6 played a big role. My daily practice up to that time had been to read a devotion or two in the morning. By "devotion" I mean a short-written entry from some periodical or book that began with a nice and encouraging Scripture text followed by a few paragraphs that usually had little to do with the Bible verse at the top. Then came a prayer and some sort of benign thought for the day. I considered that I had done my "quiet time" duty for the day and then got on with it. I'm sure these devotionals helped me in some way, but I was really just going through the devotion motions.

Somewhere in those years, I actually started reading the Bible. I remember this verse from Romans 6 stopping me dead in my tracks:

> For we know that our old self was crucified with him so that the body ruled by sin might be done away with, that we should no longer be slaves to sin—because anyone who has died has been set free from sin.

What did he just say?! Did he say I was *free* from sin? While I presented well to the public, underneath I was plagued by all sorts of sinful thoughts, attitudes, behaviors, and complex patterns of self-justification, shame, pride, and hiding, all while fiercely judging others for the same things. After reading Romans 6, I knew one of two things had to be true. Either: (1) The Bible was wrong on this point about being free from sin, or (2) I was not "getting" it—these words did not seem to describe the truth of my actual life.

This became the *Matrix*-red-pill moment of my life. I couldn't unsee what I had seen in God's Word. The Holy Spirit had planted this word in my mind as truth, and there began the long reckoning with the gospel. Jesus could no longer be an eternal life insurance policy. He would become the source and substance of a transformational life.

Romans 6 continues to teach and train my mind. Looking back over the years, I have tended to focus mostly on myself, my behavior, and my willpower even to believe the truth that I am dead to sin. Here's what's changing now. I'm starting to get this at a new level:

> Now if we died with Christ, we believe that we will also live with him. For we know that since Christ was raised from the dead, he cannot die again; death no longer has mastery over

him. The death he died, he died to sin once for all; but the life he lives, he lives to God.

The focus is not on me and my sin. The focus is on Jesus and his life. My old sin life is dead and buried in the tomb in Jerusalem. My new life is raised up and caught up in his life.

Yep, everything changed that day and is still changing . . .

The Prayer

Our Father, thank you for your son, Jesus, and the comprehensive, compelling change he brings to life. I claim it again now: I am set free from sin. I have been crucified with Christ. I no longer live, but Jesus Christ lives in me. Yes, the life I live I live by faith in the Son of God, who has loved me and given himself for me (Galatians 2:20–21). Holy Spirit, fill me and make this truth real in my actual life, over and over and over again. "Jesus, Jesus, how I trust you; how I've proved you over and over. Jesus, Jesus, precious Jesus, O for grace to trust you more."[1] Praying in Jesus's name. Amen.

The Questions

Do you believe that you are dead to sin? That sin has lost its power over your everyday life? That you are free from sin? Are you deeply grappling with the gravity of this truth?

Romans 6:11–14
32 | Why We Need a Better Bumper Sticker

> In the same way, count yourselves dead to sin but alive to God in Christ Jesus. Therefore do not let sin reign in your mortal body so

---

1. Louisa M. R. Stead, "'Tis So Sweet to Trust in Jesus," 1882.

> that you obey its evil desires. Do not offer any part of yourself to sin as an instrument of wickedness, but rather offer yourselves to God as those who have been brought from death to life; and offer every part of yourself to him as an instrument of righteousness. For sin shall no longer be your master, because you are not under the law, but under grace.

Consider This

> In the same way, count yourselves dead to sin but alive to God in Christ Jesus.

In the same way as what? Let's remember back a verse earlier:

The death he died, he died to sin once for all; but the life he lives, he lives to God. (v. 10)

We do so in the same way as Jesus did—he died to sin once for all and rose from the grave to live to God. That's how we count ourselves dead to sin and alive to God—we do it in Christ Jesus. We remember, in vivid detail and full color, the life and death and life of Jesus. We remember we are baptized into his life and death and life—which is to say we no longer live but he lives in us.

Most people simply don't get what the New Testament is saying about the Christian life. We think of it as a moral or ethical life. We approach Jesus as a moral and ethical exemplar who lived a life completely beyond ours and which would, in fact, be impossible to emulate yet we must die trying. This approach can be best summarized in three words: believe and behave. Of course, that doesn't work, which results in putting bumper stickers on our cars that say things like, "I'm not perfect, just forgiven," and "Jesus is my copilot."

Jesus tells us to "be perfect, therefore, as your heavenly Father is perfect" (Matthew 5:48). He doesn't mean perfect as we think of perfect. We think of perfect as flawless. The Bible thinks of perfect not as flawlessness but as fullness—the fullness of Jesus by the Holy Spirit. Now watch where the text takes us:

> Therefore do not let sin reign in your mortal body so that you obey its evil desires.

But how?

> Do not offer any part of yourself to sin as an instrument of wickedness,

But how?

So far this could be interpreted as saying, "Believe and behave." But then comes the secret sauce:

> but rather offer yourselves to God as those who have been brought from death to life.

The way is not believing and behaving. The way is made by beholding and becoming. This is the way of fullness. Because Jesus has wholeheartedly, unconditionally, and unreservedly offered himself to God for us, we can now wholeheartedly, unconditionally, and unreservedly offer ourselves to God for him. And then God wholeheartedly, unconditionally, and unreservedly offers the Holy Spirit to fill us with all the fullness of Jesus—for our good, for others' gain, and for the Father's glory.

And that, my friends, is perfect.

PS: Because of the pervasiveness of perfectionism, I tend to stay away from the word *perfect* altogether, but the bumper stickers we need are the ones that say, "I'm not just forgiven, I'm being made perfect," and "Jesus is my pilot."

The Prayer

My God! My Goodness! My Lord Jesus Christ. You are perfection personified, and somehow as you fill us with yourself, you bring us to perfection. Yet it is a perfection that is ever-growing and never-ending. It is a fullness that is ever admitting more of you. Holy Spirit, thank you for making us alive in Jesus—"Our living Head, and clothed with righteousness divine."[2] And so I offer my life to you, wholeheartedly, unconditionally, and unreservedly; it's all yours. And you are all mine. And because of what you did, I am now dead to sin and alive to God in Christ Jesus. Make it so more and more and more and more—from one degree of glory to the next. Praying in Jesus's name. Amen.

The Questions

Are you beginning to grasp the difference between the "believe and behave" approach and the "behold and become" approach? Are you understanding how this approach must be the beginning, middle, and end in keeping our lives consecrated to Jesus. We're dead to the old self and the old life and alive to God in Christ, meaning more life, more love, more everything that matters.

Romans 6:15–18
33 The Problem of Vertigo

> *What then? Shall we sin because we are not under the law but under grace? By no means! Don't you know that when you offer yourselves to someone as obedient slaves, you are slaves of the one you obey— whether you are slaves to sin, which leads to death, or to obedience, which leads to righteousness? But thanks be to God that, though you used to be slaves to sin, you have come to obey from your heart the pattern of teaching that has now claimed your allegiance. You have been set free from sin and have become slaves to righteousness.*

Consider This

Today's text tells us a number of things. For starters, it says we are "under grace." Remember how we talked about gravity last week and

---

2. Charles Wesley, "And Can It Be That I Should Gain," 1738.

how salvation is essentially a shifting of the center of gravity in our lives—from the gravity of sin to the gravity of grace, from the story of Adam to the story of Jesus?

Our problem comes from our very real lived experience of being caught between these two gravitational pulls—between these two masses. The gravity of Sin is dead, and yet it remains a mass that exerts pull simply by being what it is—a dead mass. The gravity of grace is alive and powerful in the Holy Spirit, and as a result, it has infinitely more power. Yet until we move fully into its sway, there is the old pull of this dead mass from our old life.

I want you to get your Romans journal or some other medium to write on and grab a pencil or pen. Now draw two circles side by side and overlapping by maybe one-third. (Yes, it's a Venn diagram). On the left side of the left circle, write the word *sin*. On the right side of the right circle, write the word *grace*. Now in the overlapping part of the circles write the word *vertigo*.

Yes, most of us, most of the time, live in vertigo. You know what *vertigo* is, don't you? It is a loss of balance or a disoriented sense of gravity, leading to dizziness and a compromised ability to walk with any stability. It is the state of being caught between the mastery of grace and the mastery of sin. We will make camp next week in the country of Vertigo (a.k.a. Romans 7), but I wanted to go ahead and put the concept in play and into the itinerary.

Did you notice the little word I sneaked into the dialogue in the last paragraph? It was *mastery*. Vertigo is the country where we learn the hard lesson that we can't achieve mastery over sin or grace. It is where we learn to follow a new master. We aren't masters who are mastering anything. We are, in fact, under mastery. We are either mastered by sin or mastered by grace. The text today makes this abundantly clear:

> Don't you know that when you offer yourselves to someone as obedient slaves, you are slaves of the one you obey—whether you are slaves to sin, which leads to death, or to obedience, which leads to righteousness?

Vertigo comes from trying to maintain two masters. Truth be told, it comes from trying to be the master of yourself—even as a Christian. Many people spend most of their life in this predictably miserable place. We try to be a Christian, and yet our old self remains held in the gravity of sin. We may salute Jesus as Lord but have never fully given him the ongoing undivided allegiance of our hearts. We are tossed to and fro by the waves of our rising and falling levels of commitment and resolve to resist our unsanctified desires or to indulge them. It is time to move beyond the slavish ways of our own self-will and sense of commitment and into a life of everyday abandoned consecration to Jesus—as Master, as Lord. This is the letting go of the old self and the taking up of the new life. Let's give Paul the last word on this today:

> But thanks be to God that, though you used to be slaves to sin, you have come to obey from your heart the pattern of teaching that has now claimed your allegiance. You have been set free from sin and have become slaves to righteousness.

The Prayer

Yes, Father, I want to move from this place of tortured vertigo and fully into the country of Grace. I am tired of sin still exercising gravity in my life and my succumbing to it. I am tired of the pattern of teaching that tells me to try harder to be better. I am weary of renewing my sense of commitment and willpower. Grace can't be another name I give my own best efforts. In fact, I am tired of endlessly asking Jesus to help me with this. I am ready to say, Jesus, have me! Yes, Holy Spirit, that is what I say: Jesus, have me! Praying in his name. Amen.

The Questions

Do you identify with the dilemma described in today's entry? Does the Venn diagram help you to see it differently? Are you caught in the middle ground of vertigo? Ready to move fully into the country of Grace?

Romans 6:19-23

34

Moving from My Commitment to Jesus's Consecration

> *I am using an example from everyday life because of your human limitations. Just as you used to offer yourselves as slaves to impurity and to ever-increasing wickedness, so now offer yourselves as slaves to righteousness leading to holiness. When you were slaves to sin, you were free from the control of righteousness. What benefit did you reap at that time from the things you are now ashamed of? Those things result in death! But now that you have been set free from sin and have become slaves of God, the benefit you reap leads to holiness, and the result is eternal life. For the wages of sin is death, but the gift of God is eternal life in Christ Jesus our Lord.*

===== **Consider This** =====

I have a friend who recently told me of her daily practice of consecration. Immediately upon waking in the morning, she kneels beside her bed and draws into fellowship with Jesus. It's a good picture of, "Wake up, sleeper, rise from the dead, and Christ will shine on you" (Ephesians 5:14). It's like she is saying, "I will let neither darkness nor daylight come between the devotion of Jesus and my desperate soul." It's become her reflexive movement of the morning: Rise up. Kneel down.

Did you catch that? Yes, I said the devotion of Jesus; not *our* devotion to Jesus but *Jesus's* devotion to us. The gospel is not that if we turn our lives around, God will love us. It is "While we were still sinners, Christ died for us" (Romans 5:8). I mean, what do we think we mean when we say Jesus loves us? It means he is devoted to us. It means he is waiting on us to wake up, every single morning, so he can shine his light in our hearts to give us the light of the knowledge of the glory of God in his very face (see 2 Corinthians 4:6; 3:12).

Paul says things like,

> In the same way, count yourselves dead to sin but alive to God in Christ Jesus. (Romans 6:11)

and

> So now offer yourselves as slaves to righteousness leading to holiness. (Romans 6:19)

He is assuming we understand the exceptional and extraordinary message of the gospel that Jesus Christ has unconditionally and unalterably given himself to us in love. If we don't understand this truth, we will mistakenly interpret it as, "Be more committed to trying harder to be better," and we will fail over and over again and ultimately settle into a life of predictable sin management.

The invitation is to respond by giving ourselves to Jesus, to belong to him wholeheartedly and unreservedly in love. This is a once and for all giving over of ourselves to Jesus and yet the real proof of whether we have really once and for all done it comes in the everydayness of doing it. Rise up. Kneel down.

It's why this prayer of consecration is prayed every single day as part of the Wake-Up Call.

Wake up, sleeper, rise from the dead, and Christ will shine on you.
   Jesus, I belong to you.
   I lift up my heart to you.
   I set my mind on you.
   I fix my eyes on you.
   I offer my body as a holy and living sacrifice to you.
   Jesus, We belong to you.
Praying in the name of the Father, and the Son, and the Holy Spirit, amen.

Jesus is jealous for us—in a good way. He knows what happens when we slide off into the abyss of sin and death. He covets life and more life for us, but we must belong to him and abide in him to receive it. Note Paul's reasoning:

> When you were slaves to sin, you were free from the control of righteousness. What benefit did you reap at that time from the things you are now ashamed of? Those things result in death!

Jesus is all about giving us a quality of life and love that does not originate in our commitment and willpower. By the Spirit, it streams from Jesus's very life in us. "Rivers of living water will flow from within [you]," is how he put it (see John 7:38).

Consecration is participation in the divine-human intermingled exchange who is Jesus himself. He gives his heart to us. He gives his mind to us. His eyes are fixed on us. He gave and gives his body for us as a holy and living sacrifice. Consecration is the mysterious, miraculous exchange of our sin for his righteousness, our brokenness for his wholeness, and our emptiness for his fullness. Through consecration, we learn to participate in the very life of Jesus by the indwelling Holy Spirit—on earth as it is in heaven.

> But now that you have been set free from sin and have become slaves of God, the benefit you reap leads to holiness, and the result is eternal life.

A final word: Eternal life does not mean "when we all get to heaven." It means heaven is now here. Eternal signifies not only duration but also quality. Eternal life is life in quantity and quality.

The Prayer

Jesus, all of this. I want all of this, and yet it all comes down to me wanting you. All of this comes with you. Would you teach me and train me in this life? Would you let that become what discipleship means in my life, even in my church? I am weary of my own ways of trying harder to manage sin. Come, Holy Spirit! I am ready for consecration, the exchange of all that is broken for all that is whole. I am ready to participate in your life here and now, for my good, for others' gain, for God's glory. Praying in Jesus's name. Amen.

The Questions

Do you feel drawn to the kind of life described in today's reading? How might you take steps toward this life? This is a visionary life—are you seeing it? What might walking into it look like? Right now? Tomorrow morning?

Week 5: Discussion Questions

Hearing the Text

Read Romans 5:18–6:23.

Responding to the Text

- What did you hear?
- What did you see?
- What did you otherwise sense from the Lord?

Sharing Insights and Implications for Discipleship

Drawing from the Scripture text and daily readings, what did you find challenging, encouraging, provocative, comforting, invasive, inspiring, corrective, affirming, guiding, or warning?

Shaping Intentions for Prayer

Write your discipleship intention for the week ahead.

6
WEEK

Romans 7:1–8:11

Romans 7:1-6

36 Facts Lead to Faith, and Faith Leads to Feelings (and Not the Other Way Around)

> *Do you not know, brothers and sisters—for I am speaking to those who know the law—that the law has authority over someone only as long as that person lives? For example, by law a married woman is bound to her husband as long as he is alive, but if her husband dies, she is released from the law that binds her to him. So then, if she has sexual relations with another man while her husband is still alive, she is called an adulteress. But if her husband dies, she is released from that law and is not an adulteress if she marries another man.*
>
> *So, my brothers and sisters, you also died to the law through the body of Christ, that you might belong to another, to him who was raised from the dead, in order that we might bear fruit for God. For when we were in the realm of the flesh, the sinful passions aroused by the law were at work in us, so that we bore fruit for death. But now, by dying to what once bound us, we have been released from the law so that we serve in the new way of the Spirit, and not in the old way of the written code.*

Consider This

Romans 6 to 8 aims to lead us out of the old country of Sin and into the new country of Grace. However, Paul is not trying to help us have some kind of warm and fuzzy experience of the grace of God. Paul is trying to help us decisively shift our mindset. He is working to help us "be transformed by the renewing of [our] mind" (Romans 12:2).

Paul is not initially concerned with our experience or our feelings. He wants us to grasp facts—how historical facts become theological facts and only later become experiential realities. This is the purpose of the analogy he gives today about the laws of marriage.

> So, my brothers and sisters, you also died to the law *through the body of Christ*. (emphasis mine)

Paul is emphatic about making the connection between the death and resurrection of Jesus and our own lives. However, he is not trying to help me have an experience but to help me reckon with a fact. The emphasis is on what Jesus has done rather than on what I must do. Jesus died to sin, fulfilled the law, was raised from the dead, and thereby won the war against Sin, sins, and death. He won—completely and totally. This is the fact. We must come to grips not with our experience but with his experience: his body, his crucifixion, his death, his burial, his resurrection, his ascension, his return. Our new reality comes "through the body of Christ."

Even now, let us declare the great mystery of our faith: Christ has died. Christ is risen. Christ will come again. Because Jesus died, we died. This is why Romans 6:11 says, "Consider yourselves dead to sin and alive to God" (ESV). Being dead to sin does not come by willpower I must exercise. No, this is a fact I must come to grips with and allow its implications to renew my mind in truth. Rehearsing again . . .

> So, my brothers and sisters, you also died to the law *through the body of Christ*,

We were held prisoners by the enemy of sin, and the law had pronounced our just sentence. And Jesus rescued us. It's right there in the text:

> that you might belong to another, to him who was raised from the dead,

And why did he do this? He did it because he loves the world he created, loves us, and is saving the world by his work extended and expressed through us. It's right there in the text:

> in order that we might bear fruit for God.

Remember, we were prisoners, enslaved in the country of Sin and Death, bound in the chaos of disordered desires, powerless to do anything about it. In other words, we were wasting our lives. It's right there in the text:

> For when we were in the realm of the flesh, the sinful passions aroused by the law were at work in us, so that we bore fruit for death.

Now see where this leads:

> But now, by dying to what once bound us, we have been released from the law so that we serve in the new way of the Spirit, and not in the old way of the written code.

I am sorry if this seems pedantic. I have become convinced we scarcely understand how the gospel actually works. We put so much stock in our own felt experience of the grace of God that we lose touch with the actual fact of the grace of God. It is not our feelings that save us. It is the facts and our faith therein. It is the ephemeral up-and-down nature of our feelings that tends to keep us in the land of Vertigo. We go there tomorrow.

The Prayer

Jesus, I belong to you. This is a fact of my life. Though you did not sin, you died to sin, once and for all. This is a fact of history and theology. Because of this, I am dead to sin and alive to God, in Jesus Christ, through the Holy Spirit. This is a fact. Holy Spirit, renew my mind with the reality of these facts. Let faith arise, and then turn that faith into real lived experience and let my feelings follow. I confess, too often I am tossed to and fro by my feelings, which leads me to fall back into sin. I am ready to get back to the facts. Praying in Jesus's name. Amen.

The Questions

Are you tracking with this line of thought today? Do you understand that the renewal of the mind precedes the renewal of felt feelings and experiences of faith?

Romans 7:7–10

37 The Dastardly Broken Brokenness of the Human Race

> *What shall we say, then? Is the law sinful? Certainly not! Nevertheless, I would not have known what sin was had it not been for the law. For I would not have known what coveting really was if the law had not said, "You shall not covet." But sin, seizing the opportunity afforded by the commandment, produced in me every kind of coveting. For apart from the law, sin was dead. Once I was alive apart from the law; but when the commandment came, sin sprang to life and I died. I found that the very commandment that was intended to bring life actually brought death.*

Consider This

I like to imagine what might have happened had God put Adam and Eve in the garden and not given them any command at all about not eating from the Tree of the Knowledge of Good and Evil. What would have happened? Sooner or later, they would have likely eaten from that tree. And what would have happened? The same thing would have happened. They would have then known the meaning of good and evil. They would have felt shame. They would have hidden their nakedness from each other. They would have hidden in the garden from God. They likely would have not known from whence all these unwanted feelings, convictions, and behaviors were coming, but they nevertheless would have been experiencing all the alienation. It would have been akin to eating something poisonous without knowing it and experiencing all the attending consequences.

I recently heard a clip from a sermon by Jackie Hill Perry sharing a fascinating insight. She pondered why God commanded Adam and Eve not to eat from the Tree of the Knowledge of Good and Evil. She suggested the following reason. God never wanted Adam and Eve to know good and evil and their difference. God only wanted Adam and Eve to know him. Wow!

So the command to not eat from the tree (which preceded the Law and yet carried the same essence) was given to protect Adam and Eve from evil rather than to deny them the experience of something good. Today's text gets at this diabolical dilemma of the frailty of human nature.

> I found that the very commandment that was intended to bring life actually brought death.

If you don't tell me where the cliff is and you don't put up any guardrails warning me, chances are I will walk right over it and fall to my death. Put up a sign that tells me to stand back ten yards and I'll walk right up to the edge and lean over.

> But sin, seizing the opportunity afforded by the commandment, produced in me every kind of coveting.

The commandment is not an exercise of the control of God over his image bearers but the care of God for us. Any parent who has small children knows this. The command "Don't play in the street" is not meant to deny the child pleasure but to protect the child from getting hit by a car. Something in a kid, however, can't stand the restriction. Give me a five-acre yard for a playground and tell me I can't play in the street and where do you think I'll play? All of this is to make the point the text makes today, which is to say the Law is a good thing, meant for our good and to protect us from death and evil, yet it had the unintended effect of multiplying sin because of the broken nature of human beings.

I'll never forget the day my across-the-street neighbor, Claude Rector, and I received the death penalty and a pardon for our bad behavior. We, of course, had been instructed not to play in the street. Our respective sidewalks mirrored each other's, leading from our respective front doors right up to the street's edge—South May Drive. In the corner of Claude's carport always sat a stack of wooden crates containing empty glass soda bottles. For whatever reason, Claude and I had the bright idea that each of us would carry a crate of those glass bottles out to the end of our respective sidewalks and proceed to take turns throwing them onto the street, breaking them into as many pieces as possible. Don't ask me why. If I know me, it was probably simply for the glory of seeing glass break. I mean, we weren't playing in the street, were we? Where does a parent even begin to deal with such dastardly behavior? I remember being caught by Alberta the babysitter (whom we feared like the plague), but I can't remember the punishment. Indeed, I think the wrath we heaped on ourselves that day was so awful that we permanently repressed it from our memories.

I'll never forget the scene, though. All that broken glass, filling up the whole street between our two sidewalks—the street we weren't supposed to be playing in—that is, for me, a fitting picture of the dastardly broken brokenness of the human race. It's amazing God would stick with us. I think I am going to finally file this story, all these years later, in the file of Romans 7.

The Prayer

Jesus, I belong to you, and I belong to you because I love you but also because outside of you I am a hopeless, dastardly mess of a human being. I know what is in me. And I know what is in you. And I want what is in you to become the defining character of what is in me. I am ready to move fully out of the tortured territory of Adam and Sin and slavery and the flesh and completely into the country of Grace and Jesus and life and love. Holy Spirit, deepen and crystallize this aspiration by the fire of your love until it is the focus of my imagination. More of Jesus. Yes, more of Jesus. It's why I'm praying in Jesus's name. Amen.

The Questions

Have you realized the fullness of the brokenness of sin inside you, or are you still minimizing, distancing from, and denying it? Are you coming to the conclusion of Jesus only and Jesus ever? How can I help you with that?

Romans 7:11–13

38 | Our Infinite Capacity for Self-Deception

> *For sin, seizing the opportunity afforded by the commandment, deceived me, and through the commandment put me to death. So then, the law is holy, and the commandment is holy, righteous and good.*
>
> *Did that which is good, then, become death to me? By no means! Nevertheless, in order that sin might be recognized as sin, it used what is good to bring about my death, so that through the commandment sin might become utterly sinful.*

Consider This

Perhaps now is a good time to recall the Venn diagram I asked you to draw in your journal last week. Again, draw two circles side by side and overlapping by about a third. On the left side of the left circle write the word *sin*. On the right side of the right circle write the word *grace*. And in the overlap write the word *vertigo*. Vertigo, you remember, is the place of a loss of balance, the confused and frustrated place of being caught and even tossed to and fro by competing gravities. These two circles might also be depicted in a vertical fashion, which lifts out a number of other insights.

Throughout Romans 5 to 8, Paul sets up the astonishing transformational shifts of the gospel: from Adam to Jesus, from slavery to freedom, and from life in the flesh to life in the Spirit. Go ahead and write Adam, slavery, and flesh on the left side of the left circle and Jesus, freedom, and the Spirit on the right side of the right circle. Again, the larger reality we are mapping is the movement from the occupied territory of Sin to the promised land of Grace. Chapter 7 depicts for us the difficult and dastardly condition of living neither fully in Sin nor in Grace but somewhere between these places.

Today's text names the nature of this between place that is both Sin and Grace and yet neither Sin nor Grace. See if you can spot the term:

> For sin, seizing the opportunity afforded by the commandment, deceived me, and through the commandment put me to death.

Yes, the word is *deceived*. Sin deceives us into believing God is not good but evil, that God is not for us but against us, and that God's will is not for our best but for our worst. Sin deceives us by telling us that what we want for our lives God does not want. Sin deceives us by convincing us God is not trustworthy. The height of deception is how sin can convince us that sin is not actually sin, that good is not actually good, and that God is not actually God. All the way back in Romans 1, we see that Sin leads human beings, created in the image of God, to trade in the truth of God for a lie and to worship created things rather than the Creator.

> Nevertheless, in order that sin might be recognized as sin, it used what is good to bring about my death.

Sin takes that which is good and uses it to bring about death.

And yes, it is the deception that creates vertigo, the place where up seems down and wrong seems right, where black and white become a thousand shades of gray, and where we become our own worst enemy. It's the place where one thing leads to another and we become lost in the deep woods with a baptismal certificate in our backpack and no idea how we got here or how to get out.

Romans 7 is not a picture of gospel life. While vertigo (in the sense we are talking) is all too common, it is not the normal Christian life. It is real to be sure, but not a required course in the curriculum of Jesus. The reason we get stuck there is because we have not sufficiently understood sin and grace and justification and repentance and Jesus and the Spirit and all we have been working our way through in these weeks in Romans.

I have learned two things today: (1) Sin is infinitely sophisticated, and (2) a human being's capacity for self-deception is almost infinite. (True even for Christians and maybe especially Christians. One need only look at the stream of high-profile Christian leaders falling into scandalous sin to grasp this.)

Sin takes that which is good and twistedly uses it to bring about our death. But God takes what is bad and graciously uses it to bring about our life. This is the story of the gospel. This is the story of Jesus.

The Prayer

Father, how we marvel at the gospel, who is Jesus Christ. Yet today I want to come to grips with my capacity not only to be deceived but to deceive myself. I simply place myself at your feet and say, Lord, have mercy on me. Bring me beyond the false piety of self-deprecation and into the place of true humility. I want to continue to renounce my self-will, my self-righteousness, and my self-assuredness, all of which are manifestations of my old, broken self, and all of which are dead and buried now. Holy Spirit, empower me to rise up into my new-creation self in Jesus Christ, alive and free, filled with all the fullness of God, and running the race marked out for me. Praying in Jesus's name. Amen.

The Questions

Are you aware of your own capacity for self-deception? What has been your experience of this condition we are describing as spiritual vertigo? How do you deal with it?

Romans 7:14–20

39

Unos, Dos, Tres, Catorce . . . ?

> We know that the law is spiritual; but I am unspiritual, sold as a slave to sin. I do not understand what I do. For what I want to do I do not do, but what I hate I do. And if I do what I do not want to do, I agree that the law is good. As it is, it is no longer I myself who do it, but it is sin living in me. For I know that good itself does not dwell in me, that is, in my sinful nature. For I have the desire to do what is good, but I cannot carry it out. For I do not do the good I want to do, but the evil I do not want to do—this I keep on doing. Now if I do what I do not want to do, it is no longer I who do it, but it is sin living in me that does it.

=== **Consider This** ===

"Hello, hello. I'm at a place called Vertigo. It's everything I wish I didn't know."[1]

Those words capture the chorus in a song of recent years by one of the greatest rock stars of our time—Paul David Hewson, also known as Bono, of the band U2.

Today's text gets us into the full melody of this place we have been calling Vertigo—this no-man's-land between the occupied territory of Sin and the promised land of Grace.

> I do not understand what I do. For what I want to do I do not do, but what I hate I do. . . . For I do not do the good I want to do, but the evil I do not want to do—this I keep on doing.

If that's not a state of vertigo, I don't know what is. Now, can we be real here?

---

1. "Vertigo," track 1 on *How to Dismantle an Atomic Bomb*, by U2 (Dublin: Island Records, 2004).

The best Romans scholars and commentators tell us Paul is not using the word *I* for himself but as though he is speaking for a hypothetical other. They also tell us Paul is not describing the Christian life in Romans 7 but rather the state of a pre-Christian person who is likely Jewish or who considers themselves a Christian while still trying to appropriate transformation by faithfulness to the Law.

For what it is worth, here is what I think. Certainly, I don't doubt Paul was dealing with Jewish members of the church who did not yet truly understand the gospel. While this particular audience is not so common among us now, I believe our churches are filled with these same kinds of people. I would call them functional Christians. They are doing their best to get with the program, follow the rules, practice the spiritual disciplines, study the Bible, raise their children to believe and behave, help people in need, give to charities, tithe to the church, go on the occasional mission trip, and otherwise do the things good Christian people do. And yet when the rubber meets the road, after years of doing this, they are still struggling with the same sin patterns, living with a scarcity mentality, judging other people for the things they most dislike about themselves, keeping score, holding grudges, blaming, shaming, withholding from, and stonewalling their spouses, and I could go on, but you get the point.

In other words, we are still living too much in the overlap of sin and grace. Sin persists as an undefeated enemy. And when functional Christians are really honest (which is not often because they mostly lack the relational context within which to do so), they say things like this:

> I do not understand what I do. For what I want to do I do not do, but what I hate I do. . . . For I do not do the good I want to do, but the evil I do not want to do—this I keep on doing.

They find themselves regressing in faith as a result of a lack of progress or because of besetting sin, infirmity, affliction, or addiction that they can't seem to beat. And I'm not trying to say what I am calling a "functional Christian" is not a Christian, because I know too many people who are definitely bonafide Christians who are living at this address. I myself have lived at this address before as a Christian and even still on occasion find myself visiting this old place. I think what I am saying, to borrow another classic lyric from Bono, is we get "stuck in a moment [we] can't get out of."[2]

The bottom line of all this "functional" faith is it has a way of leading us deeper into "Christianity" (or worse "churchianity") and often further away from Jesus himself. It's why I feel much of my ministry is to try to strip away much of functional religion and bring us back to the primitive faith of the gospel himself: Jesus.

The U2 song "Vertigo" opens with Bono's voice counting in Spanish: Unos, dos, tres, catorce. For the non-Spanish speakers, that is one, two, three, fourteen. Well, that's interesting; why from three to fourteen? This is how a master poet works, through signs and symbols. Many believe (present company included) Bono is pointing to the ancient stations of the cross. Yes, there are fourteen of them. The song ends with the lyric "Your love is teaching me how to kneel."[3]

And that's what we do at the cross, over and over and over, station after station after station. We kneel. And as we kneel with Jesus, he consecrates us.

That is the only way out of vertigo—kneeling with Jesus in consecration.

The Prayer

Yes, Lord Jesus, can we strip it all away except this simple place of kneeling with you at the cross, where we learn to behold you until we find ourselves being transformed by the renewing of our minds to become like you? Can it become that simple for us again? Indeed, your love is teaching us how to kneel. I am so weary of the vertigo, and I want to believe it will eventually go away. I am learning it leaves only to the extent that you stay. You are my balance, Jesus. Yet it doesn't look like a balanced life. It looks like the cross—not trying harder but death and resurrection. Come, Holy Spirit, and interpret this great mystery of consecration into my everyday life. Praying in Jesus's name. Amen.

---

2. "Stuck in a Moment You Can't Get Out Of," track 2 on *All That You Can't Leave Behind*, by U2 (Dublin: Island Records, 2000).

3. "Vertigo," track 1 on *How to Dismantle an Atomic Bomb*, by U2 (Dublin: Island Records, 2004).

The Questions

What insights come to you from today's entry? What are the implications of those insights? What holy intentions are beginning to form deep in your soul? How can they be enacted most simply?

Romans 7:21–25

40

The Reason We Stay Stuck in Vertigo and How to Get Free

> So I find this law at work: Although I want to do good, evil is right there with me. For in my inner being I delight in God's law; but I see another law at work in me, waging war against the law of my mind and making me a prisoner of the law of sin at work within me. What a wretched man I am! Who will rescue me from this body that is subject to death? Thanks be to God, who delivers me through Jesus Christ our Lord!
>
> So then, I myself in my mind am a slave to God's law, but in my sinful nature a slave to the law of sin.

Consider This

Previously, in Vertigo, we talked about primitive faith, which I define as the consecrated life. I see a tripartite movement in Scripture. It begins with the downward move of consecration. It moves inward to transformation. It then leads outward to impartation. And if consecration does not move toward transformation, we will find ourselves signing up for another tour of duty in the country of Vertigo.

> So I find this law at work: Although I want to do good, evil is right there with me.

While I will grant that Paul may well be talking to Jewish converts who are still trying to navigate their faith by means of the Law, I think the scenario he outlines is much larger and more common than this isolated case. Show me a real Christian who doesn't understand this . . .

> For in my inner being I delight in God's law; but I see another law at work in me, waging war against the law of my mind and making me a prisoner of the law of sin at work within me.

. . . and I'll show you a liar. ;0)

The struggle is real, and many good-hearted Christians can't seem to escape it. There is a clear reason many if not most Christians can't quite close the loop on transformation. It is because we lack the kind of relationships it takes to catalyze and sustain real transformation. Yes, we are mostly stuck in our sins because we are mostly isolated by and in our sin patterns.

While this point I am making is not featured in the text, it is assumed by the entire New Testament: The Christian faith and life is a team sport. It utterly depends on a highly relational context. It takes a church to make a real Christian. Transformation requires community.

I know many of you feel quite stuck at this point because your church is also stuck. Most churches have developed well-meaning formational programming that is long on information and study and short on transformation. We have plenty of small groups but very few places where people can show up in a way where their life, not the next great book or study, becomes the curriculum.

In my judgment (I now have significant experience in making disciples who sow for awakening) the greatest impediment we face is a lack of the kind of relationships it takes to sustain real transformation. In my work with Seedbed, we have pioneered a lost practice in the Christian faith and life. We call it banding. Eight years ago, two friends and I started Band #1, and through the process, we developed a biblically based, historically informed approach that is now bearing the fruit of transformation all over the world.[4]

---

4. Learn more about discipleship bands here: https://discipleshipbands.com/.

> So then, I myself in my mind am a slave to God's law, but in my sinful nature a slave to the law of sin.

Who is ready to put this tortured territory permanently in the rearview mirror?

And lest we forget the best word from Romans 7, concerning this place called Vertigo:

> Who will rescue me from this body that is subject to death? Thanks be to God, who delivers me through Jesus Christ our Lord!

The Prayer

Father, thank you for Jesus and for the way he banded twelve people together from the very start of his work. Thank you for the transformation we see in a person like Peter as a result of being in a band with you. Thank you that Jesus didn't give us a self-help program. I confess I have come to the conclusion that self can't help. I need Jesus and the working of the Holy Spirit through a few people around me who will go the distance. I am tired of Vertigo. I know I am hopeless alone, and I know that "Jesus and me" only gets me so far. I need "Jesus and we." Come, Holy Spirit, and open up this way before me. Praying in Jesus's name. Amen.

The Questions

So do you have a band? Are you interested in starting one? At least intrigued?

Romans 8:1–11

41

Welcome to the Second Half of the Gospel

> *Therefore, there is now no condemnation for those who are in Christ Jesus, because through Christ Jesus the law of the Spirit who gives life has set you free from the law of sin and death. For what the law was powerless to do because it was weakened by the flesh, God did by sending his own Son in the likeness of sinful flesh to be a sin offering. And so he condemned sin in the flesh, in order that the righteous requirement of the law might be fully met in us, who do not live according to the flesh but according to the Spirit.*
>
> *Those who live according to the flesh have their minds set on what the flesh desires; but those who live in accordance with the Spirit have their minds set on what the Spirit desires. The mind governed by the flesh is death, but the mind governed by the Spirit is life and peace. The mind governed by the flesh is hostile to God; it does not submit to God's law, nor can it do so. Those who are in the realm of the flesh cannot please God.*
>
> *You, however, are not in the realm of the flesh but are in the realm of the Spirit, if indeed the Spirit of God lives in you. And if anyone does not have the Spirit of Christ, they do not belong to Christ. But if Christ is in you, then even though your body is subject to death because of sin, the Spirit gives life because of righteousness. And if the Spirit of him who raised Jesus from the dead is living in you, he who raised Christ from the dead will also give life to your mortal bodies because of his Spirit who lives in you.*

Consider This

Romans 8 introduces us to what I like to call the second half of the gospel. This is the territory of great awakening. Why do I say this? Because most self-identifying Christians aren't pressing into Romans 8. They are back in Romans 5–6 territory as it relates to their faith and living more in a Romans 7–esque experience of anemic growth and arrested development.

When the church wakes up to the second half of the gospel, the world will wake up to the first half of the gospel. The world is simply not going to wake up as a result of the witness of a lot of half-baked Christians. So what about this movement from the first half of the gospel to the second half of the gospel? Here's a sketch:

The second half of the gospel is the big shift from Romans 5–6 to Romans 8:

- Jesus is my Savior to Jesus is my Lord.
- The Holy Spirit is an interesting idea to the Holy Spirit is an experiential reality.
- Deliverance from the penalty of sin to deliverance from the power of sin.
- Forgiveness for sins to freedom from sin.
- Justification by grace through faith to sanctification by grace through faith.
- Lord, you took me out of Egypt too—now take Egypt out of me.
- God as king and judge to God as Abba Father.
- True in principle to true in fact.
- Christian in name to Christian in game.
- A life of commitment to a life of consecration.
- I'm not perfect, just forgiven to I'm not just forgiven, I'm being made perfect.

Again, the big idea: When the church wakes up to the second half of the gospel, the world will wake up to the first half of the gospel. And then we will be ready to lead them into the fullness of the second half. It makes sense, doesn't it? When a person who says they are a Christian actually lives the Christian life, people take note.

The Prayer

Father, I'm ready for the second half of the gospel. I am ready for the life-giving law of the Spirit to be the governing dynamic of my life. I am ready to leave behind the country of a compromised life. Thank you, Jesus, for this life, which is your life in my life. Thank you for sending the Holy Spirit, who makes this life real. I'm ready. Praying in Jesus's name. Amen.

The Questions

Does the first half–second half framework help you make sense of how the gospel works? Are you ready for the life-giving law of the Spirit to be the governing dynamic of your life? What holds you back?

Week 6: Discussion Questions

Hearing the Text
Read Romans 7:1–8:11.

Responding to the Text
- What did you hear?
- What did you see?
- What did you otherwise sense from the Lord?

Sharing Insights and Implications for Discipleship
Drawing from the Scripture text and daily readings, what did you find challenging, encouraging, provocative, comforting, invasive, inspiring, corrective, affirming, guiding, or warning?

Shaping Intentions for Prayer
Write your discipleship intention for the week ahead.

Week 5:
Discussion Questions

Hearing the Text

Read Romans 5-8.

Responding to the Text

- What did you hear?
- What did you not hear?
- What did you experience as one, hopeful Lord?

Sharing Insights and Implications for Discipleship

Sing/say Psalm 1. Capture text into daily routines. What did you find challenging, encouraging, or worth contemplating? How to explore responses, affirming, guiding, or sending.

Shaping Intentions for Prayer

Write your discipleship intention for the week ahead.

7
WEEK

Romans 8:12–9:15

Romans 8:12–17

43 What I Do Every Morning and You Should Too

> *Therefore, brothers and sisters, we have an obligation—but it is not to the flesh, to live according to it. For if you live according to the flesh, you will die; but if by the Spirit you put to death the misdeeds of the body, you will live.*
>
> *For those who are led by the Spirit of God are the children of God. The Spirit you received does not make you slaves, so that you live in fear again; rather, the Spirit you received brought about your adoption to sonship. And by him we cry, "Abba, Father." The Spirit himself testifies with our spirit that we are God's children. Now if we are children, then we are heirs—heirs of God and co-heirs with Christ, if indeed we share in his sufferings in order that we may also share in his glory.*

Consider This

So here's the $64,000 question, at least one of them. How does one do this:

> If by the Spirit you put to death the misdeeds of the body, you will live.

I used to think it was by all manner of what is called "mortification of the flesh"—fasting to the extreme, or extreme self-denial, or even self-punishment in Jesus's name. I've tried some of that over the years, and I can truthfully say, for me, it never worked. I would feel a little bit better about feeling a little bit worse about myself, but it did nothing to curb the deeper propensities of Sin. Interestingly, the text gives no such instructions that align with what I would say is a fallen human being's distorted intuition on the subject. So again I ask, How does one do this:

> If by the Spirit you put to death the misdeeds of the body, you will live.

What if the answer is in the text immediately following?

> The Spirit you received does not make you slaves, so that you live in fear again; rather, the Spirit you received brought about your adoption to sonship. And by him we cry, "Abba, Father." The Spirit himself testifies with our spirit that we are God's children.

For almost twenty years now, my day has begun with a simple yet decisive act of immersive formation and participatory worship (usually when I'm in the shower). I give an audible voice to the Holy Spirit's cry from within my spirit, saying, "Abba, Father." Next, I transport myself through the Spirit's gift of remembrance to the ancient Jordan River and the scene of the baptism of Jesus.[1] Then I speak aloud the word of God the Father over myself, saying, "John David, you are my son—my beloved—and with you I am well pleased."

In the words of one of my favorite songs in recent years, "This is how I fight my battles." (Look up "Surrounded (Fight My Battles)—Upperroom" on YouTube. You won't be sorry.) I begin the day with a performance evaluation before the job even begins, and it has nothing to do with *my* performance. It is completely based on the identity gifted to me by the Holy Spirit, which is anchored in the Son of God. I remember at the beginning of every day that all my sins, shortcomings, and failures have no bearing on who I most truly and deeply am. I remember at the beginning of every day that I am loved, deeply loved, and not just

---

1. The word is *anamnesis*. It is the Greek word behind the word "remembrance," when Jesus lifts up the bread and cup and says, "Do this in remembrance of me" he is saying "anamnesis." It is not remembrance as recall but remembrance as re-entering the ancient reality. It is as though the distance between the present and the past is bridged by eternity now here. The past is mysteriously and even mystically brought forward as though it were happening again. I see this same dynamic at play in the baptism of Jesus, which must become our baptism, over and over and over again. It is why we call these ancient scenes of history our sacraments. They mediate the very presence of God—Father, Son, and Holy Spirit—through a way of remembrance transporting us into the ancient story; right here and right now.

a little bit but extravagantly more than I can possibly even imagine or comprehend. And nothing shreds slavery like that. I remember I am no longer a slave to my image and its management, to what anyone else thinks of me for good or bad, because I no longer live from that false self-image—buried now in baptism with Jesus—but from my true and real self, raised in resurrection life and love which is the power of Jesus.

From this place, sin is put to death because it's already dead. And from this place life flows like the river of the Spirit into the day ahead. And the day really has one agenda: Stay in the river. Because as the prophet told us, "Where the river flows everything will live" (Ezekiel 47:9).

> John David, you are my son—my beloved—and with you I am well pleased.

This is where I put into the river every single morning. Will you join me?

The Prayer

Abba Father! Abba Father! Abba Father! Thank you for your son, Jesus, and how your Spirit brings us into his life, causing our spirit to cry out those deep words of belonging. Abba Father! Thank you that we are no longer slaves but sons and daughters, buried in baptism and raised to glorious resurrection life in Jesus Christ. Thank you for your adoring, life-changing, heart-transforming, sin-crushing, everything-is-possible love for us . . . for me. I want to know you more and more until I know this more and more and then I will know everything I ever needed to know. Praying in Jesus's name. Amen.

The Questions

Try the morning routine—first say, "Abba Father." Then, speaking for God, say, "[*Insert your name*], you are my son/daughter—my beloved—and with you I am well pleased." Say it not once or twice, but would you give it a year? Or three years? This kind of transformation happens very slowly, imperceptibly even, and then one day, suddenly, you will never be the same.

Romans 8:18–25

44

When I Feel like Ruins, You See Foundations

> I consider that our present sufferings are not worth comparing with the glory that will be revealed in us. For the creation waits in eager expectation for the children of God to be revealed. For the creation was subjected to frustration, not by its own choice, but by the will of the one who subjected it, in hope that the creation itself will be liberated from its bondage to decay and brought into the freedom and glory of the children of God.
>
> We know that the whole creation has been groaning as in the pains of childbirth right up to the present time. Not only so, but we ourselves, who have the firstfruits of the Spirit, groan inwardly as we wait eagerly for our adoption to sonship, the redemption of our bodies. For in this hope we were saved. But hope that is seen is no hope at all. Who hopes for what they already have? But if we hope for what we do not yet have, we wait for it patiently.

=== Consider This ===

I want us to notice something interesting today. Romans 8 is not the resolution of Romans 7. In fact, they each contain a struggle of epic proportions. Yet the struggles couldn't be more different. Romans 7 fleshes out the struggle with sin. (See what I just did there?) Romans 8 is the struggle of redemption. Sin is waging the war in Romans 7. The Holy Spirit is waging the war of redemption in Romans 8. In other words, the movement from the realm of the flesh to the realm of the Spirit (see v. 9) is not a move from struggle to ease. Far from it. The move is from the struggle of losing to the struggle of winning. The struggle actually intensifies:

> We know that the whole creation has been groaning as in the pains of childbirth right up to the present time. Not only so,

> but we ourselves, who have the firstfruits of the Spirit, groan inwardly as we wait eagerly for our adoption to sonship, the redemption of our bodies.

Notice the word *groaning*. The word means travail. It means something like: Spirit-empowered suffering becoming physically embodied redemption. When we finally make the move from the realm of the flesh to the realm of the Spirit, we cease to be part of the problem and instead become part of the solution to the redemption of the whole world. This shift begins with our heart, moves to our home, grows into our church, and spreads into our village, town, city, state, nation, and yes, world. But note: The minute—no, the second—it happens in your heart, it has happened in the world. It comes not from trying harder but yielding more; not higher commitment but deeper consecration; not more activity but more abandonment. We will notice tomorrow who the real laborer is.

The song "Foundations" sung by my friend Tim Hughes is a truly move-mental song freighting the weight of Romans 8. Here's the chorus:

> When I feel like ruins
> You see foundations

That, my friends, is the move from the struggle of losing to the struggle of winning—"When I feel like ruins, You see foundations."

Where is the struggle boiling over in your life right now (even with sin)? Where is the suffering red-hot right now? Where does it feel like ruins right now?

This is where the blueprints are being drawn up for the building of his kingdom. Say yes to that.

The Prayer

Abba Father, it is so good to let the Spirit cry out the words of the song "Foundations" in and through my heart and mind. Thank you for Jesus, for the way he walked into the ruins of the ancient promised land and saw the foundations of your kingdom rising up. Thank you that Jesus allowed his body to become broken for us and lay like ruins in the tomb. Thank you for seeing the eternal foundations of a kingdom that will never fail. I choose this story, Jesus, your story, as my story too. And I feel this hope rising up in me, a durable hope that will not disappoint. And I sense the patient love of the Spirit settling on me. Praying in Jesus's name. Amen.

The Questions

So, about those ruins. Will you get in touch with anything that feels like ruins right now? They could be in your physical body, like cancer, or in the brokenness of your family, or in the shattering of a dream—maybe something long past but never released and healed. Put some language around it that the Spirit can grab onto. We will work it into a pleading in time.

Romans 8:26–30

45 — How the Spirit Turns Ruins into Foundations

> *In the same way, the Spirit helps us in our weakness. We do not know what we ought to pray for, but the Spirit himself intercedes for us through wordless groans. And he who searches our hearts knows the mind of the Spirit, because the Spirit intercedes for God's people in accordance with the will of God.*
>
> *And we know that in all things God works for the good of those who love him, who have been called according to his purpose. For those God foreknew he also predestined to be conformed to the image of his Son, that he might be the firstborn among many brothers and sisters. And those he predestined, he also called; those he called, he also justified; those he justified, he also glorified.*

Consider This

Ever since I first heard it in England, I've been listening to the song "Foundations." These lines stick with me:

> When I feel like ruins
> You see foundations

The song speaks—no, *cries out*—to me of the anchoring words of Romans 8:28:

> And we know that in all things God works for the good of those who love him, who have been called according to his purpose.

Some time ago, I was at the Wildfires festival. I walked across the grounds of Wiston Estate back to my room. A couple I had briefly met the day prior ran over to me and beckoned me to join their little twilight picnic group for a chat. (Did I mention it was freezing and I didn't bring the right clothes and that I was battling sickness and was bone tired?) I didn't want to do it, but something told me to sit with them. What ensued was a conversation concerning the power of the atonement, the healing mission of Jesus, and his kingdom that could only be categorized as extraordinary with a fellowship of saints who could only be categorized as exceptional.

A New Testament scene was rising up around us. One of the men in the circle, Patrick, asked if I would pray for him. It turns out he is a priest in the Church of England and an anointed healer himself. He spoke of the health crisis that emerged in his life in his early fifties. At the time of this story he was fifty-seven, and not only had his kidneys failed but they were so diseased they had to be removed, resulting in nightly dialysis at home. His physical body was in ruins. Nothing more could be done. Patrick needed a miracle of supernatural order.

> When I feel like ruins
> You see foundations

> In the same way, the Spirit helps us in our weakness. We do not know what we ought to pray for, but the Spirit himself intercedes for us through wordless groans.

I reached into my pocket and pulled out a single kernel of wheat. (I always carry seeds with me to remind me what I am doing in this world—sowing love, indeed for a great awakening.) I placed the seed in Patrick's hand. He stunned me as he put the seed in his mouth and swallowed it whole. I asked if anyone had oil. They only had wine. I asked each person to audibly affirm the ancient creed "Jesus is Lord," and then I asked each to affirm their faith in Jesus's presence to heal. I anointed Patrick with wine (a first for me), making the sacred sign of the holy cross on his forehead in the name of the Father, the Son, and the Holy Spirit. Next, I said to the circle, "Because the power of Jesus is present to heal, we need not put the emphasis on what we are doing here or our mode of prayer and intercession, but instead let us focus simply on what Jesus is doing—which is healing his son, Patrick." Because the Spirit was already interceding in wordless groans, I added, "I sense the Spirit would not have us ask for healing tonight but to instead receive healing in the name of Jesus."

I led Patrick in this simple prayer: "Jesus, I receive your healing." Then his wife and the other couple laid on hands and joined us, saying, "Jesus, we receive your healing—for Patrick." We exchanged some more words of love between us, and I departed into the night for my quarters, remembering this:

> And we know that in all things God works for the good of those who love him, who have been called according to his purpose.

And then I heard the words to that song,

> When I feel like ruins
> You see foundations.

The Prayer

Father, thank you for Jesus. And Jesus, thank you for the Holy Spirit. Sweep us up into this mystical place of prayer, where you work out your winning even through losing and even especially in losing. Praying in Jesus's name. Amen.

The Questions

As you sense faith rising in and around you, would you join voices in prayer with Patrick? "Jesus, we receive your healing." Where in your life do you see ruins taking the shape of foundations?

Romans 8:31–39

46 Yes, David, This Is for Looking At

> What, then, shall we say in response to these things? If God is for us, who can be against us? He who did not spare his own Son, but gave him up for us all—how will he not also, along with him, graciously give us all things? Who will bring any charge against those whom God has chosen? It is God who justifies. Who then is the one who condemns? No one. Christ Jesus who died—more than that, who was raised to life—is at the right hand of God and is also interceding for us. Who shall separate us from the love of Christ? Shall trouble or hardship or persecution or famine or nakedness or danger or sword? As it is written:
>
> > "For your sake we face death all day long;
> > we are considered as sheep to be slaughtered."
>
> No, in all these things we are more than conquerors through him who loved us. For I am convinced that neither death nor life, neither angels nor demons, neither the present nor the future, nor any powers, neither height nor depth, nor anything else in all creation, will be able to separate us from the love of God that is in Christ Jesus our Lord.

Consider This

As we finish Romans 8, let's ask the question, "What is Romans 8 all about?"

At first glance, we might say, "The Holy Spirit, of course!" Interestingly, the chapter mentions the Holy Spirit a whopping twenty-one times. That's not what or who it is about though, for the Holy Spirit is never about himself but always another: Jesus. Reread the chapter and you will see the whole thing is summed up in the last eleven words:

> the love of God that is in Christ Jesus our Lord.

I grew up in and around a church that had a pretty clean cross. It was not only pretty clean, but it was also pretty and clean. It wasn't until my mid-twenties that I discovered the messy cross—also known as a crucifix. I think I grew up with a bias against it, reasoning that since Jesus was risen, the cross was clean; because the tomb was empty, the cross must be too.

In my mid-twenties, I began to walk the grounds of an ancient monastery (by American standards) in the middle of Kentucky. Everywhere I turned, the crucifix confronted me. One day I bought a small crucifix statue in the gift store. It sat on my desk in my study at home. One day, when my oldest (David) was around four, he came into the study and picked up the little statue of Jesus on the cross. As he rolled it around in his tiny fingers, he asked, "Daddy, what do we use this for?" And before I could proffer some ridiculous answer, he continued, "Or . . . is it for looking at?" I knew at that moment a prophet had spoken. I said, "Yes, David, this is for looking at."

> Christ Jesus who died—more than that, who was raised to life—is at the right hand of God and is also interceding for us. Who shall separate us from the love of Christ? Shall trouble or hardship or persecution or famine or nakedness or danger or sword? As it is written:

> "For your sake we face death all day long;
> we are considered as sheep to be slaughtered."

My life in these years revealed that my cross was too clean. My life was getting messy with trouble, hardship, and persecution. I was beginning to crack into a smidgen of sharing in "the fellowship of his sufferings" (Phil. 3:10 NASB). I needed to behold more of him than I was glimpsing.

A few years later I came across a painting by Kevin Sparks called "Darkness Tries to Comprehend Light," which depicts Jesus Christ lifted up on the cross in a brutal scene of unthinkable suffering. Though it is a priceless work of art, I managed to scrape together the funds to purchase the original. As you approach the painting, you realize it's more than a painting. The cross and crucified body of Jesus are recessed—carved into the wood. And as you back away, you notice how his body is shaped like a chalice. Then you see it, the red paint, like blood coming out of the picture and across the frame at the bottom. "Yes, David, this is for looking at."

I spend time every single day just looking at it, lifting my eyes to him who is wholeness, who made himself broken so that we who are broken could be made whole, lifting my heart to him who is fullness, who made himself empty so that we who are empty could be made full.

> No, in all these things we are more than conquerors through him who loved us. For I am convinced that neither death nor life, neither angels nor demons, neither the present nor the future, nor any powers, neither height nor depth, nor anything else in all creation, will be able to separate us from the love of God that is in Christ Jesus our Lord.

That is a picture of a messy cross. Our cross is too clean, friends. Jesus is risen from the dead, and yet he is crucified. We will know him as risen only to the extent we know him as crucified. It's why the cross is the very shape of love. Our lives, with all our pain, conflicts, tragedies, brokenness, loves and losses, perplexities and persecutions, are held together by his broken body, risen and ascended to the right hand of the Father.

This is *the love of God that is in Christ Jesus our Lord*.

Yes, David, this is for looking at.

The Prayer

By the Spirit of God, our hearts keep crying out, Abba Father! Abba Father! Abba Father! No fear. No guilt. No shame. No condemnation. Only love. Only freedom. Only Jesus. We behold you, Jesus, high and lifted up, the slain Lamb of God, indeed the Lamb slain from before the foundation of the world. We are in awe of you, and the Spirit tells us you are in love with us—as you intercede on our behalf. Holy Spirit, lead us deeper into this love such that we know nothing else. Praying in Jesus's name. Amen.

The Questions

Is your cross too clean? Because I know your life is not. Are you ready for the messy cross?

Romans 9:1–5

47 | Finding Sorrow and Anguish Over My Lack of Sorrow and Anguish

> I speak the truth in Christ—I am not lying, my conscience confirms it through the Holy Spirit—I have great sorrow and unceasing anguish in my heart. For I could wish that I myself were cursed and cut off from Christ for the sake of my people, those of my own race, the people of Israel. Theirs is the adoption to sonship; theirs the divine glory, the covenants, the receiving of the law, the temple worship and the promises. Theirs are the patriarchs, and from them is traced the human ancestry of the Messiah, who is God over all, forever praised! Amen.

Consider This

I have all but ignored Romans 9–11 over the years. I say this by way of confession. I have no good excuse other than exegetical laziness. It is a hard text. Be open to its message with me today.

Paul, having come to the close of his magisterial elocution and declaration of the gospel of Jesus Christ, now faces his worst nightmare: His own people are rejecting the gospel and its God. He takes it head-on now:

> I speak the truth in Christ—I am not lying, my conscience confirms it through the Holy Spirit.

The story of the God of creation, the God of Abraham, Isaac, and Jacob, the God and Father of our Lord Jesus Christ, is the true story of the whole world. It is everyone's story. It is not, as post-Enlightenment modernity would have us believe, one choice among the pantheon of gods and religions and philosophies on offer in the marketplace. There is no other true story. Sure, there are myriad myths and philosophies and belief systems and so forth, but there is only one true story. This does not mean we need to despise, downgrade, or denigrate the multitudes of other stories and their tellers. We simply do not believe them. We believe the story of creational monotheism as revealed in the Hebrew Scriptures, which has come to its ultimate redemption and fulfillment in Jesus of Nazareth, the King of the Jews, the Lord and Messiah, Savior of the World, who was crucified and rose from the dead and ascended to the right hand of God, from which he awaits a final return to the earth, where he will consummate the new creation.

God raised up the people called Israel to declare and demonstrate this, the true story of history and eternity, of the heavens and the earth, for the blessing of the whole world and the glory and praise of God. They are the chosen stewards of this story. Look how Paul says it:

> Theirs is the adoption to sonship; theirs the divine glory, the covenants, the receiving of the law, the temple worship and the promises. Theirs are the patriarchs, and from them is traced the human ancestry of the Messiah, who is God over all, forever praised! Amen.

Unfortunately, (largely because of their leaders) the people called Israel are actively rejecting Jesus of Nazareth as the Jewish Messiah and Savior of the world. This is hitting Paul with blunt force. The grief overwhelms him because their rejection of Jesus is tantamount to a rejection of not only the whole story of God but of God himself. Paul is crushed.

> I have great sorrow and unceasing anguish in my heart.

The entire purpose of Israel, the people of God—to declare and demonstrate the story of creation and redemption for the salvation of the world and the glory of God—is on the brink of utter abrogation. Paul sees the finish line finally in sight for his beleaguered people, this long-game nation, and they are falling down in the final stretch. He can't take it. He's willing to pay the ultimate price for the team. This statement shows us the depths of Paul's despair:

> For I could wish that I myself were cursed and cut off from Christ for the sake of my people, those of my own race, the people of Israel.

So here are two questions for us as we sit now within a decade of the two thousandth year of the resurrection and ascension of Jesus Christ.

1. Do we believe that the biblical story of creation and redemption—culminating in the life, death, resurrection, and ascension of Jesus Christ and consummating in his final return—is the singularly true and controlling story of world history and eternity?
2. Do we have great sorrow and unceasing anguish over the failure of the church of our time (including ourselves) to declare and demonstrate this story for the salvation of the world and the glory of God?

My answers are *yes* and *not really*, or *maybe sort of*.

The Prayer

Abba Father! Lord Jesus Christ! Blessed Holy Spirit! Would you awaken us to the true and real story of it all? And would you forgive us for our lack of sorrow and anguish over our slumber? And would you forgive us for constantly putting our own little stories at center stage, which is to say, would you forgive us for not really believing the big story? We so desperately want to awaken to our moment in your movement. We want to play our part in this cosmic story of creation and redemption. Praying in Jesus's name. Amen.

The Questions

If your answer to question 2 is *no* or *not really* or *maybe sort of*, then are you open to sorrow and anguish over that response? Why do you think that is the case? What do you think this has to do with question 1? And what do you intend to do about it?

48 | Romans 9:6–15
A Practice Swing at Predestination

> *It is not as though God's word had failed. For not all who are descended from Israel are Israel. Nor because they are his descendants are they all Abraham's children. On the contrary, "It is through Isaac that your offspring will be reckoned." In other words, it is not the children by physical descent who are God's children, but it is the children of the promise who are regarded as Abraham's offspring. For this was how the promise was stated: "At the appointed time I will return, and Sarah will have a son."*
>
> *Not only that, but Rebekah's children were conceived at the same time by our father Isaac. Yet, before the twins were born or had done anything good or bad—in order that God's purpose in election might stand: not by works but by him who calls—she was told, "The older*

> will serve the younger." Just as it is written: "Jacob I loved, but Esau I hated."
>
> What then shall we say? Is God unjust? Not at all! For he says to Moses,
>
> "I will have mercy on whom I have mercy,
> and I will have compassion on whom I have compassion."

Consider This

The Bible is at the same time both super accessible and very complex. Sometimes the plain reading is the right reading. Other times the plain reading can obscure the better reading of the text. Romans 9 is such a text. Over the centuries, the plain reading of this text seems to point to what has come to be known in church history as the doctrine of double election predestination—the notion that God has predetermined that some will be eternally saved while many more will be eternally condemned.[2] Despite some of the smartest people in the room as its advocates, the doctrine inescapably posits a caricatured monstrosity of the God of Israel and the Father of our Lord Jesus Christ. Consider these two verses as illustrative of the point:

> Jacob I loved, but Esau I hated.

> I will have mercy on whom I have mercy,
> and I will have compassion on whom I have compassion.

All of this is too much to take on in brief reflection over morning coffee, and I am perhaps unwise for even opening the door, yet the text being what it is, I felt obliged to at least take a practice swing. We must read the verse through the lens of the whole of the Bible rather than

---

2. Learn more about predestination here: https://seedbed.com/romans-9-11-teach-calvinist-predestination/.

reading the whole of the Bible through the lens of the verse. In chapters 9–11 Paul takes us on an odyssey of biblical interpretation and understanding. For starters, he asks no fewer than twenty questions in these chapters. He quotes from the Old Testament some thirty times. The clincher, however, comes with the key term he repeats in some form eight times. That word is *mercy*.

The story of the Bible is the story of the unrelenting mercy of God—"the overwhelming, never-ending, reckless love of God," as the song says.[3] It is the story of a God who has called out to his broken image bearers from the day we hid from him in the garden of his delight to the day he cried out from the cross, "Father, forgive them, for they do not know what they are doing" (Luke 23:34), and "It is finished" (John 19:30) and every single day since. It is the story of a God who walked into the darkest night of his people and shattered the shackles of their slavery and "split the sea so we could walk right through it, drowning our fears in perfect love," as the song says.[4]

This God, our God, is on a mission that can only be described with the word *mercy*. It is a mercy so comprehensively intense that he has identified and bound himself up with us forever in history and eternity.

Say it with me, church: "For God so loved the world that he gave his one and only Son, that whoever believes in him shall not perish but have eternal life" (John 3:16).

God has thrown open the doors of his kingdom and invited everyone inside. The door is Jesus. And he ultimately chooses all who choose him. Though many will not choose him, he wills and works that all would. And he's given us one job—to participate in this most merciful work of redemption.

The Prayer

Abba Father, thank you for your mercy, which is over all your works. Thank you for giving mercy a name: Jesus. Thank you for swinging wide the door of

---

3. Cory Asbury, "Reckless Love," produced by Jason Ingram and Paul Mabury, Bethel Music, released October 27, 2017.
4. Bethel Music, "No Longer Slaves," featuring Jonathan David and Melissa Helser, produced by Ed Cash, Bethel Music, released August 21, 2015.

your kingdom to sinners like us who you are making to be saints like him. And thank you for imbuing us with Jesus's very magnetism, the Holy Spirit, who draws people to you through us. More of that, Holy Spirit! More! And thank you, like Peter said, that you are not slow to keep your promises but rather patient, "not wanting anyone to perish, but everyone to come to repentance" (2 Peter 3:9). We choose you, Jesus. I choose you. Thank you for choosing me. Praying in Jesus's name. Amen.

The Questions

Did I come down too hard on the five-point Calvinists today? If so, I apologize. They really are some of the greatest Christians in history. Are you more motivated to join the mercy mission of Jesus now?

Week 7: Discussion Questions

Hearing the Text

Read Romans 8:12–9:15.

Responding to the Text

- What did you hear?
- What did you see?
- What did you otherwise sense from the Lord?

Sharing Insights and Implications for Discipleship

Drawing from the Scripture text and daily readings, what did you find challenging, encouraging, provocative, comforting, invasive, inspiring, corrective, affirming, guiding, or warning?

Shaping Intentions for Prayer

Write your discipleship intention for the week ahead.

Week 7:
Discussion Questions

Hearing the Text

Read Romans 5:1-5.

Responding to the Text

- What did you hear?
- What do you see?
- What didn't you know or understand?

Sharing Insights and Implications for Discipleship

Reflect on the scripture and daily readings. What did you find insightful, encouraging, provocative, inspiring, hopeful, uplifting, corrective, affirming, unsettling, renewing?

Shaping Intentions for Prayer

Write your inspirational intention for the next month.

WEEK 8

Romans 9:16–10:13

Romans 9:16–21

50 On the Backstory and the Cover Story

> *It does not, therefore, depend on human desire or effort, but on God's mercy. For Scripture says to Pharaoh: "I raised you up for this very purpose, that I might display my power in you and that my name might be proclaimed in all the earth." Therefore God has mercy on whom he wants to have mercy, and he hardens whom he wants to harden.*
>
> *One of you will say to me: "Then why does God still blame us? For who is able to resist his will?" But who are you, a human being, to talk back to God? "Shall what is formed say to the one who formed it, 'Why did you make me like this?'" Does not the potter have the right to make out of the same lump of clay some pottery for special purposes and some for common use?*

Consider This

There is a backstory here in this letter. It runs both in the background and in the foreground all the time in Paul's letters. It's the story of Paul, the superstar Pharisee formerly known as Saul.

As he wrote about the hard-hearted pharaoh, I wonder if the ancient Egyptian despot served as a kind of mirror for him—of who he was becoming—under the auspices of being chosen by God. Remember, Paul cruelly persecuted the early Christians and labored passionately to crush the church (see Acts 8:1–3 and 9:1–2). To be clear, as he did these things, Paul was doing his dead level best to do the will of God. In retrospect, he must have remembered how his heart was as hard as a rock. Yet now the chief hater of the church had become its chief helper; the main detractor of Jesus of Nazareth had become his chief champion. This is so far beyond far-fetched that no one would even begin to make it up. It is impossible. And I think this is Paul's point here. Nothing is too difficult for God because God is God.

The human-bound mind wants to explain God and the ways of God in some kind of system or logic, some kind of "God has a reason for everything" system or "everything that happens is God's will otherwise God can't be sovereign" system.

> One of you will say to me: "Then why does God still blame us? For who is able to resist his will?"

Paul is saying that because God is God, all bets are off. Stop trying to figure this out. This is beyond your pay grade. He is giving his readers the first-century translation of, "Shut up."

> But who are you, a human being, to talk back to God?

As Paul writes, he wrestles with God. He wants his people, the Jews, to be in on the cover story. They are, after all, God's chosen people. Yet Paul knows God is doing something much larger here than just the Jews, and he knows he himself is a sign and symbol of it—the chief sinner becoming the chief saint. That's the cover story: It's all about Jesus. Paul's life is now an illuminated backstory.

Here's the kicker: Paul thought he was the main story before he met Jesus. Now he knows his life is a backstory for the great cover story of Jesus. He never imagined it because it was beyond imagination. Paul is now running through the Rolodex of the whole Bible. With the Jews now seated as his jury, who can he call on here? Jeremiah! Yes, Jerry—what would he say?

> "Shall what is formed say to the one who formed it, 'Why did you make me like this?'" Does not the potter have the right to make out of the same lump of clay some pottery for special purposes and some for common use?

God will be God, so we must let God be God. So here's the gospel in it all: Though we can't understand God, we can trust God. Why? Because God is just? Sure. There is more, though. Because God is mercy. And is this just some sort of divine philosophy we are supposed to accept?

Nope. God has spoken a final word that will save the whole world—it's the Word that brings divine justice and divine mercy together into the eternal revelation of divine love: Jesus.

Many of us are still waiting to trust God until we understand God; when all the while, the truth is, we will not understand God until we trust him. This is the very meaning of faith. And this gospel of Jesus will come to us by faith or not at all. Remember, faith is not believing something you aren't sure is true, as in you just have to "accept it on faith." No, faith is trusting in the reality of someone you are coming to believe is The Truth. This is how your life becomes a backstory in the greatest cover story of all time.

Yes, Jesus.

The Prayer

Abba Father, thank you for Jesus, your perfect image in human flesh. Thank you that if we have seen Jesus, we have seen you. Thank you for not standing outside of your creation but coming into it and not only coming into the created reality but into us, your image bearers. Jesus, we belong to you. Holy Spirit, would you impart to us the mind of Jesus that we might think thoughts after God? Help us not to wait to understand before we trust, but rather to trust and then find we understand. You are the Potter. We are the clay. We trust you, God, with our lives. Praying in Jesus's name. Amen.

The Questions

Are you growing in your understanding that you are not the potter but the clay? How are you awakening to a deeper faith—beyond the same old blind acceptance of something you don't understand?

Romans 9:22–29

51

The First and Last Question of Any Theologian Worth Their Salt

> What if God, although choosing to show his wrath and make his power known, bore with great patience the objects of his wrath—prepared for destruction? What if he did this to make the riches of his glory known to the objects of his mercy, whom he prepared in advance for glory—even us, whom he also called, not only from the Jews but also from the Gentiles? As he says in Hosea:
>
> "I will call them 'my people' who are not my people;
>   and I will call her 'my loved one' who is not my loved one,"
>
> and,
>
> "In the very place where it was said to them,
>   'You are not my people,'
>   there they will be called 'children of the living God.'"
>
> Isaiah cries out concerning Israel:
>
> "Though the number of the Israelites be like the sand by the sea,
>   only the remnant will be saved.
> For the Lord will carry out
>   his sentence on earth with speed and finality."
>
> It is just as Isaiah said previously:
>
> "Unless the Lord Almighty
>   had left us descendants,
> we would have become like Sodom,
>   we would have been like Gomorrah."

Consider This

Something deep within every single one of us wants to be God, even if we don't want to admit it. At least we want to sit in that seat from time to time. This is the Achilles' heel of being the image bearers of God. We have enough of the stuff of God in us that we think we can do the job better than God—and clearly we can do it better than the guy driving the car next to us. We think we know best.

As a result, we are all amateur theologians, desperately trying to understand what is happening in us and to us and all around us, and to make sense of it, and yes, to explain it to each other. For better or for worse, we are all doing theology all day every day, believers or not, willfully or unconsciously. Theology, or grasping after the logic of God, is our native language. Again, when you are made in the image of God, it's what you do.

So Paul is doing theology with the Roman church about this matter of the Jews and their future and his agonizing hope concerning such. And because we have time yet to discuss all this business, I would like us to take a minute to get some altitude, look down, and admire his method. For starters, notice the three-word opener, which he repeats again in the same paragraph:

> What if God . . . ?

It is a beautiful way to open a conversation, isn't it? *What if God . . . ?* Ponderous, open, invitational, and yes, humble. When it comes to conversations about God, beware the NIDs and the SIDs: That's shorthand for the "never in doubt" and the "seldom in doubt." They mean well, but they are plagued with insecurity, and as a result, they can't risk faith, so they opt instead for an overconfident certainty. Faith pursues another outcome: clarity.

> What if God . . . ?

Notice also how Paul pursues clarity. He's not building on the philosophical constructs of Aristotle, Socrates, or Plato. Nope. For Paul, it's Abraham, Isaac, and Jacob. He works from Scripture as not only his foundation but also his four walls and infinitely vaulted ceiling. The story of Scripture serves like his stained glass: The windows through which all light enters and is filtered—and the lenses through which he sees and interprets all of life and the world, both history and eternity. He called on Sarah and Rebekah, Pharaoh and Jeremiah, and today it's Hosea and Isaiah. Paul knows this story upside down and inside out. He knows it not like an academic remembers facts and data but like an old man remembers his life story with all its twists, turns, and surprising transformations. The story of Scripture is the substance of his memory and the source of his imagination.

> What if God . . . ?

That's the starting place, isn't it? It can lead to questions like, "How might God be working in this challenging situation or that intractable dilemma?" and "What might God be saying to us in this moment of opportunity and possibility?"

> What if God . . . ?

It's also the ending place, isn't it? On this point, no one says it better than Isaiah. We will give him the last word today.

> "For my thoughts are not your thoughts,
>   neither are your ways my ways,"
> declares the Lord.
> "As the heavens are higher than the earth,
>   so are my ways higher than your ways
>   and my thoughts than your thoughts." (Isaiah 55:8–9)

The Prayer

Abba Father! Indeed, we know this—your thoughts and ways are not our ways and thoughts. Your ways are higher, deeper, longer, and infinitely wiser than we can imagine or even comprehend. And yet you have written them down in a book, through a thousand stories that are one story, and all of it perfectly finished and beautifully fulfilled in Jesus. Come, Holy Spirit, and teach us to ask this question: "What if God?" and to let the question permeate our stories, big and small. I want to be that kind of theologian. I want to live a "What if God" life. Praying in Jesus's name. Amen.

The Questions

What if God . . . ? Where are you asking this question these days? How is the story of Scripture becoming like the stained glass windows of your life?

Romans 9:30–33

52 | Jesus and Paul Would Not Have Been Friends

> What then shall we say? That the Gentiles, who did not pursue righteousness, have obtained it, a righteousness that is by faith; but the people of Israel, who pursued the law as the way of righteousness, have not attained their goal. Why not? Because they pursued it not by faith but as if it were by works. They stumbled over the stumbling stone. As it is written:
>
> > "See, I lay in Zion a stone that causes people to stumble
> > and a rock that makes them fall,
> > and the one who believes in him will never be put to shame."

Consider This

I had a BFO (blinding flash of the obvious) today.

Paul and Jesus were the same age (give or take a few years). They grew up in different places—about five hundred miles apart. They were both Jews. Relatively speaking, Paul was born into privilege; Jesus into relative poverty. Jesus—as the second person of the Trinity—was by order of magnitude in another category than Paul, and yet both were otherwise ordinary first-century men.

Perhaps most significantly, both of these men had the same purpose, goal, and ambition in life. They both wanted to see Israel, the people of God, fulfill their God-ordained role as the light of the world. They both wanted the kingdom of God to come on earth as it is in heaven. They wanted to see scriptural holiness spread across the land—the glory of God filling up the whole earth as the waters cover the sea.

Both of these men were men of the Law—of Torah. They both knew the story of God inside out and upside down. But that's about where their similarities end. When it came to their method, their approach couldn't have been any more different. Let's say Jesus and Paul would not have been friends. Paul led the movement within Judaism that believed the way forward was 100 percent straight legalistic obedience to the Law. We should probably point out the absurdity of this approach at the outset here. Let's call it a legalistic observance of the Law that paraded as self-righteous obedience. Jesus despised this approach.

It is oversimplifying it to say this, and yet it is right. Paul set out to keep the Law with a legalistic observance.

> But the people of Israel, who pursued the law as the way of righteousness, have not attained their goal. Why not? Because they pursued it not by faith but as if it were by works.

Jesus came to fulfill the Law with overwhelming love. Paul would have considered Jesus totally irrelevant. Jesus would have considered Paul very dangerous.

And in the irony of all ironies, Paul's approach to the Law would nail Jesus to the cross.

Nope, Jesus and Paul would not have been friends . . . until they were.

They never met before Jesus was crucified. They met after Jesus was raised from the dead and ascended into heaven (Acts 9). Suffice it to say, after this meeting on that fated road to Damascus, Paul and Jesus would become best friends forever. In a move that would stun paupers and princes, Paul came over to team Jesus, and the rest is history. Talk about overwhelming love—Jesus picked Paul, his biggest detractor and the fiercest enemy of the church, to quarterback his team.

> "See, I lay in Zion a stone that causes people to stumble
> and a rock that makes them fall,
> and the one who believes in him will
> never be put to shame."

Jesus, the great stumbling block for the Jews (and all seeking to attain righteousness and salvation by their own efforts), became the solid rock on which Paul would stand and beckon the Jews (and everyone else) to stand with him. All other ground is sinking sand.

The Prayer

Abba Father! What a story! What a Savior! Jesus, we belong to you. We love this story because it is all at once too good to be true and yet it is the truest story ever told. You took the chief of sinners, who prided himself as the paragon of righteousness, and turned him into a preeminent saint. You took your worst enemy and turned him into your best friend. What a Savior! It raises my confidence in what you might be able to do in my life, with me, even me. I just want to stand on this rock and bow in awe for now. Praying in Jesus's name. Amen.

The Questions

Had you ever thought of Jesus and Paul as being the same age, contemporaries of their time, with many similarities and yet massive differences? What observations do you make about this fact of history?

Romans 10:1–4

53

On the Most Dangerous Condition in the World

> Brothers and sisters, my heart's desire and prayer to God for the Israelites is that they may be saved. For I can testify about them that they are zealous for God, but their zeal is not based on knowledge. Since they did not know the righteousness of God and sought to establish their own, they did not submit to God's righteousness. Christ is the culmination of the law so that there may be righteousness for everyone who believes.

Consider This

There are three words you don't want to hear together, and you certainly don't want to hear them spoken of you: zeal without knowledge.

There is a way of doing the work of God that destroys the work of God. That way is called "zeal without knowledge."

It is a way of working for God instead of working with, in, and through Jesus by the power of the Spirit. You believe every word of the Bible, do your dead level best to do what it says, support all God's causes, take bold stands for Jesus, earn perfect attendance Sunday school pins and all sorts of other spiritual merit badges, put Jesus bumper stickers on your car, wear the T-shirts, and basically tick all the religious boxes. And all of this is done in the name of Jesus, and yet it gives Jesus a bad name. How?

Because it is without knowledge. This word *knowledge* (*epignosis* in the Greek) is not what we may think. It is not knowledge as in knowing a lot of stuff about God. It means something more like "contact knowledge." It is knowledge gained through relationship. Yes, it means "knowing." It means knowing someone rather than knowing about someone.

To say a person is infected with zeal without knowledge is to say they are someone who needs to be in control. This is what Paul says about the

Jews here. Paul knew them because he was them. This is why sin does not originate from immorality but insecurity. People who need to be in control are insecure people. We know them because we are them.

This is what is behind works-based righteousness: not diligence but insecurity, not the surrendered-ness of faith in God but fear that creates the need to be in control of everything, including God, while being seen as acting in the name of God. This is the nature of zeal without knowledge. And if you know anything about Paul's track record, you know it is deadly.

The people who carry "zeal without knowledge" will put the mission of God over the people and would-be people of God all day long. They will believe they are loving God as they do damage to people, and all in the name of Jesus. They will callously neglect family and friendships for the cause and consider that they have a higher calling than all that. It is one of the most diabolical evils in life.

Zeal is not bad. It can be a good quality. Knowledge, in the sense of knowing God, is infinitely better. Zeal for God without intimately knowing God is the worst. Zeal for God issuing forth from the intimate knowledge of God leads to the most beautiful thing in the world: faith moving in love.

Permit me the rare word of radical candor here today. If you think you may be even remotely infected with zeal without knowledge, get to the floor as fast as you can and repent with a prayer something like this:

Lord Jesus Christ, Son of God, have mercy on me a sinner.

Why such a grave tone today? Here's why. In the very words of Jesus,

> Many will say to me on that day, "Lord, Lord, did we not prophesy in your name and in your name drive out demons and in your name perform many miracles?" Then I will tell them plainly, "I never knew you. Away from me, you evildoers!" (Matthew 7:22–23)

Zeal without knowledge. Yep. That's what he's talking about.

The Prayer

Abba Father! We come before you with open hearts, asking you to search us and know us. Would you ferret out our need to be in control and expose it as sin to us? Our controlling nature defies faith and destroys love. It kills relationships, destroys churches, and paralyzes the movement of your kingdom. We renounce our need to control, and we confess it as the source of our self-righteousness and our deceived plot to save ourselves. Yes, Jesus, this is as old as time and as current as this moment. Have mercy on us, Lord Jesus. Have mercy on us. Cleanse us, Holy Spirit, and renew a right spirit in us. Praying in Jesus's name. Amen.

The Questions

Do you tend to be a controlling person?

54

Romans 10:5–9

The Simple, Succinct, Sophisticated, Comprehensive Gospel

> *Moses writes this about the righteousness that is by the law: "The person who does these things will live by them." But the righteousness that is by faith says: "Do not say in your heart, 'Who will ascend into heaven?'" (that is, to bring Christ down) "or 'Who will descend into the deep?'" (that is, to bring Christ up from the dead). But what does it say? "The word is near you; it is in your mouth and in your heart," that is, the message concerning faith that we proclaim: If you declare with your mouth, "Jesus is Lord," and believe in your heart that God raised him from the dead, you will be saved.*

Consider This

Could it really be this simple?

> If you declare with your mouth, "Jesus is Lord," and believe in your heart that God raised him from the dead, you will be saved.

I mean, isn't there something more—actually, isn't there a ton more to the Christian faith than just declaring something with your mouth and believing something in your heart? No. This is the whole tamale.

> If you declare with your mouth, "Jesus is Lord," and believe in your heart that God raised him from the dead, you will be saved.

But what about all the people who say the words and claim to believe but their lives are a living denial of the whole thing—you know, the so-called nominal Christians? It's not our concern. We are not the judge. They will answer for themselves.

> If you declare with your mouth, "Jesus is Lord," and believe in your heart that God raised him from the dead, you will be saved.

The words of the verse we must concern ourselves with are as follows: "you . . . your mouth . . . your heart . . . you."

> If you declare with your mouth, "Jesus is Lord," and believe in your heart that God raised him from the dead, you will be saved.

The gospel—yes, the whole gospel, in all its essence and entirety—comes down to these two historical and eternal verities:

1. Jesus is Lord, and
2. God raised him from the dead.

Sure, there is much more to say, but this is enough said. Jesus is Lord. It's a pretty comprehensive creed. God raised him from the dead. It's a massively sophisticated reality.

> If you declare with your mouth, "Jesus is Lord," and believe in your heart that God raised him from the dead, you will be saved.

These aren't magic words, but they are profoundly miraculous. They carry the very freight and essence of salvation, which is the deep restoration of the human race and the healing of all creation.

> If you declare with your mouth, "Jesus is Lord," and believe in your heart that God raised him from the dead, you will be saved.

Are you ready? Again or for the very first time?
Declare with your mouth: Jesus is Lord.
Believe in your heart: God raised him from the dead.
Wake up, sleeper, rise from the dead, and Christ will shine on you! Come on!

The Prayer

Abba Father! Thank you that the gospel is by faith and that your righteousness is revealed. Thank you that it does not depend on our works or our getting it right but on our faith and our making it real. Yes, thank you for a righteousness that is from first to last by faith alone in these simple and comprehensive facts: Jesus is Lord. God raised him from the dead. Come, Holy Spirit, and rivet this reality into my heart of hearts. Break me out of the broken realm of my own imaginings and into the expansive space of faith and freedom and real-life salvation. Praying in Jesus's name. Amen.

The Questions

Does this stripping back to the foundation of things encourage you or frustrate you? How are you dealing with this word today?

55 | Romans 10:10–13

Everyone Who Calls on the Name of the Lord Will Be Saved

> For it is with your heart that you believe and are justified, and it is with your mouth that you profess your faith and are saved. As Scripture says, "Anyone who believes in him will never be put to shame." For there is no difference between Jew and Gentile—the same Lord is Lord of all and richly blesses all who call on him, for, "Everyone who calls on the name of the Lord will be saved."

Consider This

Let's remember what Paul is up to in chapters 9–11 if not the whole letter; okay, if not all his letters. Paul is doing what he's always been doing. Paul is trying to bring Scripture to its fulfillment by building up the ancient people of God into a nation favored and blessed by God—through whom the whole world would be blessed. Paul is trying to spread scriptural holiness across the land so that the glory of God could be known in the world as the waters cover the sea.

In other words, Paul is trying to save the world.

But he's not trying to do it through the government or some sort of globalizing movement. That was what Rome was up to (a.k.a., the Pax Romana, the Roman peace). It was decidedly a "peace through strength" approach with Caesar as lord and king. You see, in those days to say Jesus is Lord was not to express a warm and fuzzy pious spiritual sentiment. It was a seditious political declaration. Understand, though, the point was not to overthrow the government and take down Rome. The point was to sow the seeds of the gospel into tiny communities of people who would become seedbeds of great awakening—demonstration plots of the kingdom of heaven on earth.

Paul is trying to encourage the tiny community of Christians (a.k.a. the church Jesus is building) in Rome. Remember, we are talking about a hundred people or so in a city of a million.

Let's remember something here, though. This is the long game. Paul is not building his churches to somehow stand against the gates of Rome. Paul, like Jesus, is building his church to withstand the gates of hell. Remember this day with Jesus at Caesarea Philippi?

> "But what about you?" he asked. "Who do you say I am?"
>
> Simon Peter answered, "You are the Messiah, the Son of the living God."
>
> Jesus replied, "Blessed are you, Simon son of Jonah, for this was not revealed to you by flesh and blood, but by my Father in heaven. And I tell you that you are Peter, and on this rock I will build my church, and the gates of Hades will not overcome it." (Matthew 16:15–18)

It's why Paul says this:

> For it is with your heart that you believe and are justified, and it is with your mouth that you profess your faith and are saved.

So how do you save the world? The same way you eat an elephant—one bite at a time. Paul's first and major challenge here in Rome is that of uniting the Jews and the gentiles into one big happy family under the lordship of Jesus Christ. Most of the Jews seem to remain intractably stuck in a centuries-old ditch known as works-based righteousness. Paul is trying to bring them into the gospel of Jesus, which is faith-based righteousness. It is not a righteousness one earns as a *right* but receives as a *gift*. This is difficult for self-sufficient and control-oriented people, then and now.

> For there is no difference between Jew and Gentile—the same Lord is Lord of all and richly blesses all who call on him,

Paul is bringing all the people to the foot of the cross, where the ground is level, at the feet of Jesus, where . . .

> Everyone who calls on the name of the Lord will be saved.

The Prayer

Abba Father! Thank you for the simple gospel, who is your son, Jesus, our Messiah. Everyone who calls on the name of the Lord will be saved. This means no one is left out or excluded. Holy Spirit, would you impress on us the meaning of everyone? And would you teach me, again, what it means to "[call] on the name of the Lord"? I want this to become my way of life, calling on the name of the Lord. Praying in Jesus's name. Amen.

The Questions

Are you growing in your basic understanding of what this letter is all about? Have you been guilty of ignoring the bigger story and just trying to glean some tidbits for yourself—you know, just trying to get something relevant for your life? Are you seeing how the bigger story matters?

Week 8: Discussion Questions

Hearing the Text

Read Romans 9:16–10:13.

Responding to the Text

- What did you hear?
- What did you see?
- What did you otherwise sense from the Lord?

Sharing Insights and Implications for Discipleship

Drawing from the Scripture text and daily readings, what did you find challenging, encouraging, provocative, comforting, invasive, inspiring, corrective, affirming, guiding, or warning?

Shaping Intentions for Prayer

Write your discipleship intention for the week ahead.

9
WEEK

Romans 10:14–11:32

Romans 10:14-15

57 — How Feet Become Beautiful

> *How, then, can they call on the one they have not believed in? And how can they believe in the one of whom they have not heard? And how can they hear without someone preaching to them? And how can anyone preach unless they are sent? As it is written: "How beautiful are the feet of those who bring good news!"*

Consider This

How do feet become beautiful?

I don't like feet. I never have. Not my feet. Not your feet. They are inglorious, gangly, grungy, dirty, sweaty, and smelly. And yet . . .

> How beautiful are the feet of those who bring good news!

Still, the words *feet* and *beautiful* don't readily go together, do they?

But feet are important, essential, vital, and necessary. It turns out feet may play the most important role in the kingdom of Jesus. Feet are the logistics of the gospel. Note the logistical logic of today's text:

> How, then, can they call on the one they have not believed in? And how can they believe in the one of whom they have not heard? And how can they hear without someone preaching to them? And how can anyone preach unless they are sent?

A person calls on Jesus because
A person believes in Jesus because
A person heard about Jesus because
A person told them about Jesus because
A person was sent to embody and share Jesus because
Feet. Therefore . . .

> How beautiful are the feet of those who bring good news!

So feet become beautiful when they are sent to carry the gospel of Jesus. The gospel moves on foot or it doesn't move. I love how God sent his Son to the earth at a time before motorized vehicles. Jesus walked. As he walked, the gospel moved, because he was and is and evermore shall be the gospel. A phrase in the Seedbed Sower's Creed gets at this and translates it to our lives:

Because Jesus is good news and Jesus is in me, I am good news.

As we walk, Jesus walks in, with, and through us. As we walk, the gospel moves.

> How beautiful are the feet of those who bring good news!

And maybe, just maybe, this is why Jesus washed those first disciples' feet. Sure, it had to be done, but it was more than that, wasn't it?

He came to Simon Peter, who said to him, "Lord, are you going to wash my feet?"
Jesus replied, "You do not realize now what I am doing, but later you will understand."
"No," said Peter, "you shall never wash my feet."
Jesus answered, "Unless I wash you, you have no part with me." (John 13:6–8)

I think I'm finally beginning to understand, at least more than I did. Jesus, by his cleansing presence, takes the most unseemly part of me and makes it the most beautiful. He consecrates our feet to be sent as the carriers of his presence, power, and love to the world, from our neighborhood to the nations. It is how he has part with us and we with him.

> How beautiful are the feet of those who bring good news!

And that's how feet become beautiful.

The Prayer

Abba Father! We simply marvel at your son, Jesus. He did something so surprising and so unseemly two thousand years ago, and we are still growing in our understanding of it all. Lord Jesus, thank you for washing their feet, and in washing their feet you washed the feet of all who would ever follow you. Come, Holy Spirit, and fill us up to fullness, making us the sent ones of Jesus. Give us beautiful feet to carry the good news of his presence everywhere we go to everyone we meet every single day. Praying in Jesus's name. Amen.

The Questions

So how about your feet? Are they beautiful yet? How might they become so? Are you aware that you carry the presence of Jesus—with your feet? How might that awareness grow? Do you grasp that you are sent by Jesus?

Romans 10:16–21

58 | How to Not Miss Jesus

> *But not all the Israelites accepted the good news. For Isaiah says, "Lord, who has believed our message?" Consequently, faith comes from hearing the message, and the message is heard through the word about Christ. But I ask: Did they not hear? Of course they did:*
>
> > *"Their voice has gone out into all the earth,*
> > *their words to the ends of the world."*
>
> *Again I ask: Did Israel not understand? First, Moses says,*
>
> > *"I will make you envious by those who are not a nation;*

> *I will make you angry by a nation that has no understanding."*
>
> And Isaiah boldly says,
>
> *"I was found by those who did not seek me;*
> *I revealed myself to those who did not ask for me."*
>
> But concerning Israel he says,
>
> *"All day long I have held out my hands*
> *to a disobedient and obstinate people."*

Consider This

As you might imagine, I get a lot of reader mail. I've shared my cell number before, so I also receive my share of text messages. This week a reader I affectionately call "Aunt Bette" sent me this text:

> WHAT IF the Israelites had not rejected the cornerstone but by faith received all given to them? Where would we be?

I texted her back with this reply: "Aunt Bette, we would be (as they say back home) in tall cotton!"

This is the wrestling match Paul is having in today's text. Why didn't Israel get it? He need only look in the mirror and ask himself. These guys were expert Bible readers, and yet they didn't have a clue. How did they miss Jesus?

Maybe I have just answered my own question. Sometimes, maybe more than I want to admit, expert Bible readers don't have a clue.

Think about it. Jesus, the very Word of God in human flesh, came face-to-face with expert Bible readers, and they didn't know him from Adam. It was clear from the start he read the Bible very differently than they did. It's almost like they were reading a different Bible altogether. It's why Jesus prayed prayers like this:

> At that time Jesus said, "I praise you, Father, Lord of heaven

and earth, because you have hidden these things from the wise
and learned, and revealed them to little children. Yes, Father,
for this is what you were pleased to do." (Matthew 11:25–26)

This should frighten us. We, too, can read the Bible and miss Jesus. These first-century Jewish readers of Scripture were certain they had it right, and yet had it exactly wrong. They were highly controlling, very certain, and as a result, highly prideful and very obstinate people. We can be the same, can't we? If the "people of God" can completely miss God, it stands to reason the "followers of Jesus" can completely miss Jesus.

So how do we not miss Jesus?

The answer is tucked right into his prayer: Become like children. He does not mean whimsically childlike as some have said, and he certainly did not mean childish. It means to become humble. No matter how advanced you think you are in your studies or in your faith, here is the secret to not missing Jesus:

Be small.

Live humbly.

Stay hungry.

All of this comes together in what is all at once the saddest and happiest text in Scripture:

He came to that which was his own, but his own did not receive him. Yet to all who did receive him, to those who believed in his name, he gave the right to become children of God. (John 1:11–12)

Be small. Live humbly. Stay hungry.

The Prayer

Abba Father! Thank you for this invitation to be small, to live humbly, and to stay hungry. Jesus, this is who you were and are and evermore shall be. You, the most towering figure of history and eternity, allowed yourself to become small. You humbled yourself and became obedient to death, even death on a cross. And you showed us what it looks like to live hungry—that we do not live by bread alone but by every word that comes from the mouth of God. Come, Holy Spirit, and emblazon these words on our hearts and our minds. I want to be small. I want to live humbly. I want to stay hungry. Praying in Jesus's name. Amen.

The Questions

Are you learning to pursue clarity instead of certainty? Are you learning to let go of your need to be in control? Are you learning that small is the new big? And that humility is the new superpower? And that hunger is the secret to staying filled? Let's go!

Romans 11:1–10

59

The Apostle Paul: Converted or Completed?

> I ask then: Did God reject his people? By no means! I am an Israelite myself, a descendant of Abraham, from the tribe of Benjamin. God did not reject his people, whom he foreknew. Don't you know what Scripture says in the passage about Elijah—how he appealed to God against Israel: "Lord, they have killed your prophets and torn down your altars; I am the only one left, and they are trying to kill me"? And what was God's answer to him? "I have reserved for myself seven thousand who have not bowed the knee to Baal." So too, at the present time there is a remnant chosen by grace. And if by grace, then it cannot be based on works; if it were, grace would no longer be grace.
>
> What then? What the people of Israel sought so earnestly they did not obtain. The elect among them did, but the others were hardened, as it is written:
>
> > "God gave them a spirit of stupor,
> >   eyes that could not see
> >   and ears that could not hear,
> > to this very day."

> And David says:
>
> "May their table become a snare and a trap,
>   a stumbling block and a retribution for them.
> May their eyes be darkened so they cannot see,
>   and their backs be bent forever."

Consider This

Growing up I always thought of Jesus as a Christian. I thought this so much I didn't even recognize he was a Jew. In fact, I thought of Christianity as a completely new thing, distinct from Judaism. It felt like Jesus and grace were a massive left turn from the Old Testament. After all, the story is in the *New* Testament, right?

And Paul—why do we speak in terms of Paul's (or Saul's) conversion? Shouldn't we be talking about Paul's completion? Because of this "conversion" language, I always thought of Paul's blinded-by-the-light Damascus-road experience as another left turn. This was the plan for Paul from the beginning, before one day of his life came to be—that he would become a Jew in the way of Jesus and the gospel of the fullness of the fulfillment of God.

On the Damascus road Paul reached the natural conclusion of his life as a Jew. This is the intended way for all Jews. (I suppose I could understand a gentile conversion much more, but a Jewish conversion really doesn't make sense. This is the path for all human beings made in the image of God.)

So why do we call it Paul's conversion? Does the Bible call it this? Or is that just the uninspired headings? When we call it a conversion, we imply that Paul was on the wrong path. And Paul had indeed taken a wrong turn. Truth be told, he was on the ancient path of the people of God. Paul, as a Jew, was on his way to becoming what a Jew most truly was meant to be—on the path of what the earliest followers of Jesus called "the Way." And the Way had always been the Way. After all, Abraham is the father of the Way, isn't he? Nothing new here, right? The ancient way was totally fulfilled but not new.

Only now am I beginning to see it differently. Jesus was not new.

How can the second person of the Trinity be new? Jesus always was. Far from plan B or a last-ditch effort, he was always the plan. He would be the fulfillment of the pre-ancient plan of God to redeem the world he created. The long and winding road was always the plan.

Jesus is the path for the whole human race. This is what Paul is up to in today's text, particularly in this section on the future and destiny of the Jews. He is showing us how the Way threaded through the whole story from beginning to end. It was always there, just as the end of Romans 11 indicates:

> For from him and through him and for him are all things.
> To him be the glory forever! Amen. (Romans 11:36)

The Prayer

Abba Father! How we thank you for Jesus, who was and is and is to come, the image of the invisible God and the firstborn over all creation. Thank you that he is the Lamb slain from before the foundation of the world. I confess I have often seen Jesus as a divine plot device. Thank you for opening my eyes to begin to fathom that he is the whole story. For from him and through him and for him are all things. To him be the glory forever! Praying in Jesus's name. Amen.

The Questions

Have you, like me, thought of Christianity as a left turn from Judaism? How about Paul's "conversion" as an exceptional moment rather than as the intended norm?

Romans 11:11–16

60 | The Cheer I Can't Stop Chanting

> *Again I ask: Did they stumble so as to fall beyond recovery? Not at all! Rather, because of their transgression, salvation has come to the*

Gentiles to make Israel envious. But if their transgression means riches for the world, and their loss means riches for the Gentiles, how much greater riches will their full inclusion bring!

I am talking to you Gentiles. Inasmuch as I am the apostle to the Gentiles, I take pride in my ministry in the hope that I may somehow arouse my own people to envy and save some of them. For if their rejection brought reconciliation to the world, what will their acceptance be but life from the dead? If the part of the dough offered as firstfruits is holy, then the whole batch is holy; if the root is holy, so are the branches.

Consider This

As my two daughters came up through middle and then high school, I had the occasion to go to a lot of volleyball games. I often found myself out on the court as a line judge. I remember one particular game in a tournament where I learned a new cheer I will never forget. Don't worry though, as a line judge I wasn't cheering, at least not vocally. Our team fell behind in the tournament's elimination game. In the absence of sanctioned cheerleaders, one of the kids took it upon themselves to rally the crowd.

The kid shouted out, "I!" And a few of the other kids echoed, "I!"

Then the kid shouted, "I believe!" More kids joined in the echo, "I believe!"

Then the self-appointed cheerleader again, "I believe that!"

The now growing echo of not just the kids but the crowd, "I believe that!"

The cheerleader, now in full cadence, shouted, "I believe that we!"

The crowd, now in full cadence, echoed, "I believe that we!"

Doing my best to remain impartial while attending to my duties as a line judge, I had become mesmerized by this cheer. Where was it going? I had never heard anything like it in all my days as a sports fan.

Then came the capstone words to finish the now full-bore chant:

I believe that we will win!

And the chanting, cheering throng echoed it over and over:

> I believe that we will win!
> I believe that we will win!
> I believe that we will win!
> I believe that we will win!
> I believe that we will win!

"And your point?" you are undoubtedly asking.

By the time we are eleven verses into chapter 11, this kind of chant is essentially what Paul is doing. Take a look:

> Again I ask: Did they stumble so as to fall beyond recovery? Not at all! Rather, because of their transgression, salvation has come to the Gentiles to make Israel envious.

Translation: *I believe that we will win!*

> But if their transgression means riches for the world, and their loss means riches for the Gentiles, how much greater riches will their full inclusion bring!

Translation: *I believe that we will win!*

> For if their rejection brought reconciliation to the world, what will their acceptance be but life from the dead?

Translation: *I believe that we will win!*

It's like Paul's conceding that the Jews had blown the lead. They were way behind. But their apparent losing out was now being used by Jesus to swing wide the door for the gentiles to come in. And the gentiles coming in was now being used by Jesus to motivate the Jews to get back into the game. Look! Already, they were a small and growing remnant—

> If the part of the dough offered as firstfruits is holy, then the whole batch is holy; if the root is holy, so are the branches.

This remnant would persist and grow, and soon enough the whole team would be back on the field. This was a temporary setback.

> Again I ask: Did they stumble so as to fall beyond recovery?

Translation: *I believe that we will win!*

It's a good word—a good six words. Far from some kind of arrogant triumphalism, these six words form a powerful declaration of faith. How can Paul be so confident? Because he knew the victory had already been signed, sealed, and delivered with the resurrection of Jesus. It was now just a matter of time.

As that lone kid rose to begin the chanting cheer, and the individual "I" took on the powerful and collective "We," the tide turned in that middle school gym. Our team mounted a comeback fit for *SportsCenter*. We won! And we went on to win the whole tournament.

Church, we will win because Jesus has won. Gentiles and Jews of every nation, tribe, and tongue, together with every creature "in heaven and on earth and under the earth" (Revelation 5:13), chanting these words in a thousand languages:

Jesus Christ is Lord!
I believe that we will win!

The Prayer

Abba Father! We join today with the angels and the archangels and the elders and the living creatures, saying, "Holy! Holy! Holy Lord! God of power and might. Heaven and earth are full of your glory!" We cry out with the great communion of saints above, "Hosanna in the highest!" We cry out with the church below, all over the world, "Blessed is he that comes in the name of the Lord!" Bring in the gentiles! Bring in the Jews! Come, Holy Spirit, and usher in the kingdom of Jesus in all its fullness as we cry out, "He is risen! He is risen indeed!" Indeed, we declare, "I believe that we will win!" Praying in Jesus's name. Amen.

The Questions

Are you ready and willing to become that single cheerleader in the gymnasium of faith (a.k.a. the church of Jesus Christ) in your neighborhood? Are you ready to join the rising chorus of those all over the world already chanting the victory of faith?

61 Romans 11:17–24
Halftime with the Apostle Paul

> *If some of the branches have been broken off, and you, though a wild olive shoot, have been grafted in among the others and now share in the nourishing sap from the olive root, do not consider yourself to be superior to those other branches. If you do, consider this: You do not support the root, but the root supports you. You will say then, "Branches were broken off so that I could be grafted in." Granted. But they were broken off because of unbelief, and you stand by faith. Do not be arrogant, but tremble. For if God did not spare the natural branches, he will not spare you either.*
>
> *Consider therefore the kindness and sternness of God: sternness to those who fell, but kindness to you, provided that you continue in his kindness. Otherwise, you also will be cut off. And if they do not persist in unbelief, they will be grafted in, for God is able to graft them in again. After all, if you were cut out of an olive tree that is wild by nature, and contrary to nature were grafted into a cultivated olive tree, how much more readily will these, the natural branches, be grafted into their own olive tree!*

Consider This

I've never seen it this way before, but I may be onto something for once. Paul is turning the eleventh chapter of Romans into a full-fledged pep rally. Today it is going to be a straightaway halftime talk with the team.

Throughout the whole letter, Paul has worked to forge a one-team mentality between what heretofore had been understood as two teams: the Jews and the gentiles.

Remember, one of the main things Paul is trying to do in all his letters is to solve particular problems these fledgling churches were facing. This matter of the Jews and the gentiles was one of the most pressing and pervasive problems across all the churches. These communities were rife with prejudices, power dynamics, and petty infighting. Like Jesus, Paul knew a house divided could not stand, so his first and last order of business was to bring communities to the level ground of the cross of Jesus, where the Holy Spirit could raise them into demonstration plots of resurrection power.

Reading Romans, we get the sense of two opposing (or at least conflicted) sides. It was more like the Jews versus the gentiles rather than the Jews *and* the gentiles. This church in Rome—or rather these little churches in Rome—was somewhat segregated. Remember the story. Emperor Claudius had expelled all Jews from the city several years before, and with the rise of Nero, many of the Jews were making their way back. A number of them had belonged to the church before the exile, and now they were coming back into those same churches, which had become largely gentile. These Jews would have felt displaced, like they were coming back home but no longer really belonged.

It's kind of the same when an old-line traditional church begins to take on the shape of what the old saints derisively call "the church of what's happening now." Hymns bow to choruses, hymnals surrender to screens, and pipe organs move aside for guitars. Next thing you know, the drummer will be wearing holey jeans! You know what I'm talking about. The gentiles are taking over! But I digress . . .

Paul now turns the halftime talk into a bit of what back home we call a "talking to" with the gentiles. He tells these gentiles in no uncertain terms they are the "newcomers." The Jews were there first by a long shot. The gentiles have been "grafted" into the olive branch, which was the Jewish people. Though the Jews had been originally drafted, the gentiles were now being grafted. (I couldn't resist!) The Jews were the roots. The gentiles were the shoots.

> Do not consider yourself to be superior to those other branches.
> If you do, consider this: You do not support the root, but the
> root supports you.

Next, Paul boldly rebukes these apparently braggadocious gentiles.

> Do not be arrogant, but tremble.

Then Paul plays the proverbial ace of spades. He reminds them who owns the game and all the game pieces:

> For if God did not spare the natural branches, he will not spare you either.

> Consider therefore the kindness and sternness of God: sternness to those who fell, but kindness to you, provided that you continue in his kindness. Otherwise, you also will be cut off.

It's halftime. Coaches never give game balls at halftime. This is a long game. This game belongs to God. And the name of the game is mercy.

The Prayer

Abba Father! We thank you, for you are kind. We thank you, for you are mercy. We thank you, for you are patient. We thank you, for you are love. We thank you, for you are Jesus. And we thank you, for you are the Holy Spirit, who brings Jesus into us and us into you. We confess, our tendency can be arrogance rather than trembling. Come, Holy Spirit, and bring us back into the vision of your kindness that leads us to repentance. Bring us back into the vision of your mercy that leads us to humility. Bring us into the fullness of Jesus, who fills everything in every way for the glory of it all. Praying in Jesus's name. Amen.

The Questions

Are you grasping all the insider-outsider dynamics at play in this letter and in these churches and all the pride and prejudice floating around? Do you see how arrogance and entitlement creep in so easily? How do you see these dirty dynamics at play in your community?

62 | Romans 11:25–32
Why God Is Not Fair Is a Good Thing

> I do not want you to be ignorant of this mystery, brothers and sisters, so that you may not be conceited: Israel has experienced a hardening in part until the full number of the Gentiles has come in, and in this way all Israel will be saved. As it is written:
>
> > "The deliverer will come from Zion;
> > he will turn godlessness away from Jacob.
> > And this is my covenant with them
> > when I take away their sins."
>
> As far as the gospel is concerned, they are enemies for your sake; but as far as election is concerned, they are loved on account of the patriarchs, for God's gifts and his call are irrevocable. Just as you who were at one time disobedient to God have now received mercy as a result of their disobedience, so they too have now become disobedient in order that they too may now receive mercy as a result of God's mercy to you. For God has bound everyone over to disobedience so that he may have mercy on them all.

Consider This

Are you still hearing the cheer-filled chant? Because Paul is not letting up.

I believe that we will win!

He has this belief on the sure evidence of revelation—God's decree.

> As it is written:
>
> "The deliverer will come from Zion;
> he will turn godlessness away from Jacob.
> And this is my covenant with them
> when I take away their sins."

Meanwhile, back at the ranch, the gentiles were flocking into the kingdom. It was too much for the average Jew—a kingdom with a crucified Messiah and anybody and everybody gets in who will "declare with your mouth, 'Jesus is Lord,' and believe in your heart that God raised him from the dead" (Romans 10:9).

The Jews suffered from a condition common to people of privilege. They were born on third base and thought they hit a triple. These Jews had a birthright. They had paid their dues. They were, after all, God's chosen people. How dare God go allowing in all this riffraff. As the saying goes, this place is going to you-know-where in a handbasket.

That condition of the Jews is common to the human race. It's called pride. And my friends, pride is the hardness of the heart. Hear Paul's opener again today:

> I do not want you to be ignorant of this mystery, brothers and sisters, so that you may not be conceited: Israel has experienced a hardening in part until the full number of the Gentiles has come in.

The Jews did have a birthright, but it did not amount to a claim on God. It's why Jesus famously told Nicodemus, a Jew, he would have to be "born again." It's why Jesus famously told the poor who flocked to him, "Blessed are the poor in spirit, for theirs is the kingdom of heaven" (Matthew 5:3).

This gospel is pure gift or it is nothing. This gospel requires simple faith or nothing. Check your birthright at the door. Check your church attendance at the door. Check your good behavior at the door. Check your accomplishments and accolades and credentials and qualifications at the door. All of that might matter and have some value in some places, but it has less than no value at the only door that ultimately matters. Yes, check your anything and everything else but "Jesus Christ is Lord and God raised him from the dead" at the door.

To be clear, this is not about getting into heaven when you die. This is right here, right now kingdom of Jesus stuff. This is the "on earth as it is in heaven" reality or it is no reality at all.

This reminds me of the time Jesus told the story about the farmhands. The farmhands lined up for work one day, and the farmer came early and hired a crew. The farmer came back at nine and noon and three and finally at five, each time hiring an additional crew to join the field labor. He agreed to pay them all a denarius for the day's work. In the evening, he lined them up beginning with the last ones to join the crew so he could pay them first. Right down the line from the last crew to the first, he paid them all the same wage. The early risers were furious. This was not fair in their eyes. They grumbled.

> "These who were hired last worked only one hour," they said, "and you have made them equal to us who have borne the burden of the work and the heat of the day." (Matthew 20:12)

I love what the farmer told them.

> But he answered one of them, "I am not being unfair to you, friend. Didn't you agree to work for a denarius? Take your pay and go. I want to give the one who was hired last the same as I gave you. Don't I have the right to do what I want with my own money? Or are you envious because I am generous?" (Matthew 20:13–15)

Here's my translation:

I'm not fair. Be very glad I'm not fair. I am so much better than fair. I am merciful.

The Prayer

Abba Father! This word about your fairness challenges me to the core. Thank you that mercy is unfair. Thank you that grace is unfair. Now and forever no one has any claim on you. It is your mercy and your grace, and you can do with it as you please. Holy Spirit, would you help me understand this at the deepest level? I want to know Jesus through and through, inside and out, upside down. I want to know this truth in my bones, in my deepest self. Grace me to be humble, poor in spirit, meek, and even holy. Praying in Jesus's name. Amen.

The Questions

Do you question this notion that God is not fair? Do you see how his being merciful is so much better, albeit on a completely different plane? And do you see how justice aligns with mercy and even how God's justice is a very different reality than human notions of fairness?

Week 9: Discussion Questions

Hearing the Text

Read Romans 10:14–11:32.

Responding to the Text

- What did you hear?
- What did you see?
- What did you otherwise sense from the Lord?

Sharing Insights and Implications for Discipleship

Drawing from the Scripture text and daily readings, what did you find challenging, encouraging, provocative, comforting, invasive, inspiring, corrective, affirming, guiding, or warning?

Shaping Intentions for Prayer

Write your discipleship intention for the week ahead.

Week 9:
Discussion Questions

Hearing the Text
Read Romans 16:1-27.

Responding to the Text
- What did you notice?
- What did you feel?
- What did you hear or sense from the Lord?

Sharing Insights and Implications for Discipleship
Looking at the Scripture text and our daily readings, what did you find challenging, encouraging, provocative, comforting, convicting, inspiring, provoking, affirming, guiding, or warning?

Shaping Intentions for Prayer
Write your disciplinship intentions for the week ahead.

10
WEEK

Romans 11:33–13:5

Romans 11:33–36

On Lighting Fires in the Sky

> Oh, the depth of the riches of the wisdom and knowledge of God!
>   How unsearchable his judgments,
>   and his paths beyond tracing out!
> "Who has known the mind of the Lord?
>   Or who has been his counselor?"
> "Who has ever given to God,
>   that God should repay them?"
> For from him and through him and for him are all things.
>   To him be the glory forever! Amen.

Consider This

Growing up in the First United Methodist Church of Dumas, Arkansas, meant a number of things, but one thing you could set your clock by. Every single Sunday, every single month, of every single year, there were two songs we would sing at almost precisely the same moments in every single worship service. The songs were called the "Gloria Patri" and the "Doxology."

Here's the first one:

> Glory be to the Father, and to the Son and to the Holy Ghost.
> As it was in the beginning, is now and ever shall be.
> World without end, Amen. Amen.[1]

And here's the second:

> Praise God from whom all blessings flow.
> Praise Him all creatures here below.

---

1. "*Gloria Patri*," traditional hymn, 2nd century.

Praise Him above ye heavenly host.
Praise Father, Son and Holy Ghost.
Amen.[2]

If you look up the word *doxology* in the dictionary, you get this:

doxology: a liturgical formula of praise to God

Those 936 Sundays of my growing up years were just that, "a liturgical formula of praise to God." Time to stand up and sing. Now sit down. Now greet your neighbor. Now stand back up and sing. Now sit down. Now listen and try to stay awake.

And I thank God for all 936 times. They formed me. They shaped my liturgical memory so that in time I would cultivate a doxological imagination. These songs gave me the muscle memory of looking up, forgetting any shred of myself, and singing words exclusively unto the God of Gods.

Here's how I define doxology. A doxology is a series of combustible words that, when lit, create fire in the sky. To sing a doxology—to really sing it—is to light a fire in the sky and allow yourself to become caught up in it.

That's what happened to Paul in today's text. After a stunning eleven-chapter exploration and exposition of the glory of the grace of Abba Father in the Lord Jesus Christ through the incredible Holy Spirit, he could do nothing else. He lit a fire in the sky and got caught up in it.

Read today's text again if you don't believe me. You will get caught up too.

Yep, he lit a fire in the sky and got caught up in it.

Doxology—this is what I want to happen in my life every single day. And I want it to happen in yours. What we do in church on Sundays is good, my friends, but it's only practice. It's developing the muscle memory for the real game of the other six days.

It would take another thousand words to explore this fully, but isn't that the very essence of the day of Pentecost—the day he lit a fire in the sky over our heads and caught us up in himself?

---

2. Thomas Ken, "Doxology," 1674.

I often talk about carrying seeds, and I will continue. But I think we should also carry matches.

The Prayer

Abba Father! "Oh, the depth of the riches of the wisdom and knowledge of God!" (Romans 11:33). Thank you for sending your Son, for lighting up the sky with the glory of grace and mercy, for lighting up our lives with all the possibilities of the kind of faith that moves mountains and the kind of love that raises the dead. Thank you for showing us who we actually are and are meant to be in Jesus. Thank you for sending your Spirit to make our lives burn for the glory of you alone. Praying in Jesus's name. Amen.

The Questions

Do you ever find yourself sporadically breaking into doxology? Would you like to? What would it mean for you to start carrying matches to light these kinds of fires in the sky along the path of an ordinary week?

Romans 12:1

65 | The Jesus Manifesto

> *Therefore, I urge you, brothers and sisters, in view of God's mercy, to offer your bodies as a living sacrifice, holy and pleasing to God—this is your true and proper worship.*

Consider This

In the 1900s—1994 to be exact—I was about to begin seminary at Asbury Theological Seminary in Wilmore, Kentucky. I left behind two jobs, one as a youth pastor and the other as a part-time lawyer. On my cross-country drive to Kentucky, I decided it was time to get serious about "rememberizing" Scripture. My starting point? You guessed it—Romans 12. And I named Romans 12 the Jesus Manifesto because it's a declaration of the Christian life.

> Therefore . . .

Anytime you see *therefore* in Scripture (or any other literature for that matter), you should ask, What is it "there for"? *Therefore* is the great theological hinge of Romans. Chapters 1–8 unfold the glorious contours of the gospel of grace. Chapters 9–11 delve into the "I believe that we will win" conundrum of Israel. And chapter 12 tells us what Romans 1–11 are there for. *Therefore* opens the door.

"I urge you" comes from the Greek word *parakaleo*. This is a compound word, and some English equivalents of the second half of the word are: to admonish, exhort, entreat, beg, beseech, encourage, strengthen, summon; and last but not least—to call. And that's just the *kaleo* part. The *para* part means "to come alongside." So when we read, "I urge you" (I *parakaleo* you), it has the effect of Paul walking right up to us, putting his arm around our shoulders, and loudly declaring (brace for it),

Wake up sleeper! Rise from the dead, and Christ will shine on you!

> Brothers and sisters . . .

Notice that Paul doesn't say, "Jews and gentiles." His reality is that of a family. The goal is not to help Jews and gentiles get along or even to become friends. He calls them "brothers and sisters" because the people of God are united into one family.

> offer your bodies as a living sacrifice.

If the Bible has a call to action, it is contained in this phrase. But I see at least two dilemmas here. For a long time, I read it like this: "offer your bodies as living *sacrifices*." My favorite Bible translation—the 1984 New International Version—even translated it that way. But as I see it, they overlooked something important. The Greek word for "sacrifice" is singular, which the latest version of the NIV got right. You're seeing the issue, aren't you? The text says, "Offer your *bodies* as a living *sacrifice*." Bodies (plural). Sacrifice (singular). Many bodies—one sacrifice. The New Testament church, the one Jesus is building, is not a bunch of independent individuals running around trying to make Jesus famous. This is a great challenge for the church today—to become the body of Christ living the will of God rather than millions of individuated bodies doing their own thing in God's name.

The other dilemma is easier to spot. The phrase "*living* sacrifice" is an oxymoron (e.g., jumbo shrimp, working vacation, smartphone). A sacrifice, by nature, is dead. In baseball, when a batter hits a pop fly to the outfield and the base runners advance to the next base, it is deemed a sacrifice. The batter is out. When a soldier jumps on a hand grenade to save others' lives, it is deemed a sacrifice. The soldier is dead. What on earth is a *living* sacrifice? How on earth does a sacrifice live?

> in view of God's mercy

This magical, miraculous phrase contains the rationale for all of Romans, if not the whole Bible. Without the active, living vision of God's mercy, the best you can hope for is religious activism by human willpower. You will endlessly try harder to do better and slowly convince yourself you aren't as bad as your neighbor and soon start phoning it in, embracing a tepid faith leading to a mediocre life.

But that's not you.

You live in the view of God's mercy.

The mercy of God is a vision of the eternal, endless outreach of the almighty God of heaven and earth—offering the gifts of mercy and grace to all who would freely receive. Yes, the mercy of God is Jesus Christ offering himself freely and fully to broken sinners like every single person who has ever lived. Far from some sort of transaction of salvation, it is the gift of relationship that gives us the ability to live a transformed and transformative life.

In view of that, the invitation is this: Offer your bodies as a living sacrifice. In light of God's offering to us, let us now make an offering of ourselves to God.

The Prayer

Abba Father! Thank you for Jesus, the original living sacrifice, the crucified and risen Lord of heaven and earth. He has shown us how to live the life of a living sacrifice. Holy Spirit, fill us with the courage to walk this path of faith—to die before we die so we might truly live while we are alive and then gloriously onward into eternity! I want to be a living sacrifice, in union with my brothers and sisters in Jesus, for the glory of God. Praying in Jesus's name. Amen.

The Questions

How do you live "in view of God's mercy"?

66 Romans 12:2
Why the Mind Must Lead the Heart in the Matter of Transformation

> *Do not conform to the pattern of this world, but be transformed by the renewing of your mind. Then you will be able to test and approve what God's will is—his good, pleasing and perfect will.*

Consider This

As the Jesus Manifesto (a.k.a. Romans 12) continues, I get further and further behind. Friends, this is an endless all-you-can-eat buffet and then some. Let's stay connected, though, to the root call to action:

> Therefore, I urge you, brothers and sisters, in view of God's mercy, to offer your bodies as a living sacrifice, holy and pleasing to God—this is your spiritual act of worship. (Romans 12:1 NIV 1984)

We often think of "spiritual" acts of worship as being invisible things like deep, warm, and fuzzy feelings toward God that lead to going to church and singing and stuff like that. To be sure, these are good, but the text doesn't go there. The most spiritual thing in the world is the most physical—the offering up of our very flesh-and-bones bodies. Real worship is an everyday, ground-level phenomenon. If verse 1 is the call to action, verses 2–21 show us what it looks like when the "view of God's mercy" (v. 1) becomes a visionary life. The essential movement happens in verse 2:

> Do not conform to the pattern of this world, but be transformed by the renewing of your mind.

What is the pattern of this world? In short, it is the mind of Adam. Remember our earlier work on this point on "The Soundtrack of the Gospel" (Romans 5:18–21) with the A form: ∧? The renewed mind is the mind of Christ, depicted in the V form: ∨. When someone is transformed from the mind of Adam to the mind of Jesus, their life becomes a burning fire of glory to God. Look where this goes:

> Then you will be able to test and approve what God's will is— his good, pleasing and perfect will.

As we let go of the old self corrupted by Adam and take hold of the new self transformed by Jesus Christ, we become less and less self-centered and more and more Christ-centered. And as we become more and more Christ-centered, we become more and more others oriented. We become living beacons of the love of God for other people. Put simply, this is the will of God: to love God with all we've got and to love others as we love ourselves. This is a visionary life, a life inspired by the mercy of God. In this miraculous way of life, the more you give, the more you have to give.

A final point: Note how we are talking about the mind rather than the heart here. Both matter deeply, but in the matter of transformation, the mind is the real battleground. The heart will follow the mind. The focus of our eyes will follow the fixation of our hearts. And all of this is the pathway to the offering of our physical bodies. It's why every single day in our prayer of consecration we lift our hearts to Jesus and we set our minds on him. Then we fix our eyes on him, and the offering of our body follows. All of this is what it means to be spiritual, to worship God in spirit and truth. This is what we were made for. This is who we are becoming. And yes, this is the long game we are playing.

The Prayer

Abba Father! Thank you that you have made us to worship you and in worshiping you to be delivered from self-centeredness and set free to love others. Thank you for the visionary life of mercy of your Son, Jesus. Open the eyes of our hearts to really see Jesus. Holy Spirit, would you continually orient and reorient us into this life for which we were made, not to conform to the pattern of the world but to be transformed by the renewing of our minds? We want this for ourselves and our families and our churches, for the sake of our neighbors and our cities and the world. Praying in Jesus's name. Amen.

The Questions

Who in your past and present life would you identify as living this visionary and inspired life of love for God and others, being beacons of the miraculous mercy of God? Do you want to become this kind of person? Are you getting a better picture of how real transformation happens with the mind, heart, eyes, and body?

Romans 12:3–21

67

On Keeping the Cart Behind the Horse

For by the grace given me I say to every one of you: Do not think of yourself more highly than you ought, but rather think of yourself with sober judgment, in accordance with the faith God has distributed to

> each of you. For just as each of us has one body with many members, and these members do not all have the same function, so in Christ we, though many, form one body, and each member belongs to all the others. We have different gifts, according to the grace given to each of us. If your gift is prophesying, then prophesy in accordance with your faith; if it is serving, then serve; if it is teaching, then teach; if it is to encourage, then give encouragement; if it is giving, then give generously; if it is to lead, do it diligently; if it is to show mercy, do it cheerfully.
>
> Love must be sincere. Hate what is evil; cling to what is good. Be devoted to one another in love. Honor one another above yourselves. Never be lacking in zeal, but keep your spiritual fervor, serving the Lord. Be joyful in hope, patient in affliction, faithful in prayer. Share with the Lord's people who are in need. Practice hospitality.
>
> Bless those who persecute you; bless and do not curse. Rejoice with those who rejoice; mourn with those who mourn. Live in harmony with one another. Do not be proud, but be willing to associate with people of low position. Do not be conceited.
>
> Do not repay anyone evil for evil. Be careful to do what is right in the eyes of everyone. If it is possible, as far as it depends on you, live at peace with everyone. Do not take revenge, my dear friends, but leave room for God's wrath, for it is written: "It is mine to avenge; I will repay," says the Lord. On the contrary:
>
> "If your enemy is hungry, feed him;
>   if he is thirsty, give him something to drink.
> In doing this, you will heap burning coals on his head."
>
> Do not be overcome by evil, but overcome evil with good.

Consider This

I know, I know. I have packed a ton into Romans 12, the Jesus Manifesto. Even though we are covering a lot of verses, a massive message is bursting through. Here's the message: The success of verses 3 through 21 depends entirely on the secret of verses 1 and 2.

Here's what I would like to say about verses 3 through 21. There are—count them—thirty-nine commands in these nineteen verses of Scripture. This text must have more command density than even the Old Testament Law. Note, though, this is not so much of a "thou shalt not" set of commands as it is a "you must do" set of marching orders.

You and I have no hope of obeying these thirty-nine commands across these nineteen verses (vv. 3–21) unless we grasp verses 1 and 2. More plainly: Verses 3 through 21 are the cart. Verses 1 and 2 are the horse. I will repeat those first two verses yet again for emphasis.

> Therefore, I urge you, brothers and sisters, in view of God's mercy, to offer your bodies as a living sacrifice, holy and pleasing to God—this is your true and proper worship. Do not conform to the pattern of this world, but be transformed by the renewing of your mind. Then you will be able to test and approve what God's will is—his good, pleasing and perfect will. (Romans 12:1–2)

The great problem of modern Christianity is we want to skip straight to the wrong question, "What are we supposed to do?" and right over the most crucial matter, "Who are we intended to become?" In other words, we want to put the cart before the horse. The text couldn't be any clearer. It is "being transformed" that leads to the ability to "test and approve" and ultimately do the will of God.

The first verse reveals the path of consecration. The second verse reveals the way of transformation.

The major point of verses 3 through 21 comes in verse 9, "Love must be sincere" or two little Greek words: *anupokritos agape* that could be translated as "real love." *Real*, as in not fake or feigned. *Love* as in the love of Jesus. Everything else in the chapter, the letter, the New Testament, the whole Bible is a commentary on these two words: *real love*. Once we live into verses 1 and 2, the ability to live out verses 3 through 21 flows like an unstoppable river. And yes, everywhere the river flows, it brings life to dead places.

Real love. You see, the issue for people like us is not so much no love as it is fake love. Fake love is another way of saying self-interested or self-serving love, which is not really love at all but manipulation. The concept here comes from the theater and points to actors playing parts rather than real human beings being their true selves.

Real love. This is who we are becoming in Jesus Christ, and this is how we are becoming it—through Jesus Christ in us. Real love is the simplest and most satisfying reality in life. It is the most comprehensively creative force in the universe. It is not hard, but it is demanding as it requires significant unlearning and letting go of former ways of being (i.e., the patterns of this world). In the end, it will be all that matters, which means it's all that really matters right now. It's why we keep saying, "Wake up, sleeper, rise from the dead, and Christ will shine on you!"

The Prayer

Abba Father! Real love! That is who you are. That is who Jesus is. That is who the Holy Spirit is. Not soft and fuzzy and sentimental love but real hardcore love. Your love goes beyond feeling. It transcends emotion. It is unconditional and unwavering—even for our enemies, even in the face of hatred. It is impossible for us yet already realized in Jesus. Come, Holy Spirit, and realize this real love in us through Jesus in us. Keep us at the altar of consecration, that we might walk the path of transformation and that we might live a life of real love for the glory of it all. Praying in Jesus's name. Amen.

The Questions

Are you grasping how verses 1 and 2 are the key to the rest of Romans 12? Are you seeing that *real love* is not possible for us to exercise until we know we are *really loved* (as in living life in view of God's mercy)?

Romans 13:1–3

68

Why We Must Pay Our Taxes

> Let everyone be subject to the governing authorities, for there is no authority except that which God has established. The authorities that exist have been established by God. Consequently, whoever rebels against the authority is rebelling against what God has instituted, and those who do so will bring judgment on themselves. For rulers hold no terror for those who do right, but for those who do wrong. Do you want to be free from fear of the one in authority? Then do what is right and you will be commended.

=== **Consider This** ===

We read Romans 13 with its admonition to be subject to the government and our thoughts run to names like Bush and Obama, or Trump and Biden. And we scratch our heads. Let me share with you the real head-scratcher of today's text: *Nero*.

The name alone evokes terror and horror. There are corrupt leaders and then there are wicked leaders. Nero was undoubtedly both. Nero is the one who would blame the Christians for the burning of Rome and subject them to persecutions perhaps unrivaled in all of history. This is the one who would nail Christians to crosses, cover them in tar, and then light them on fire to illuminate his gardens at night. Nero is reportedly the emperor who crucified the apostle Peter.

Let's be clear, though. At the time of this letter, things had not yet progressed to the levels of evil that they ultimately would. Something tells me Paul foresaw it and wanted to avoid it, so he was taking a more measured approach here.

> Let everyone be subject to the governing authorities, for there is no authority except that which God has established.

Paul was not trying to set up a theology or philosophy of church and state here. Romans chapter 13 is among the most perilous texts in the Bible because of the ways it is prone to abusive misinterpretation (e.g., see the divine right of kings).

The most critical thing to point out about what Paul says here is this: We aren't being admonished to "obey" the government but to be "subject to the governing authorities." We must obey Jesus Christ alone. Submission and obedience are two different things.

As we read further, we will discover this is about taxes. Paul is telling the Christians they must pay their taxes. Like Jesus, Paul is saying to render to Caesar what is Caesar's (which are the taxes owed) and render to God what is God's—which is not everything else but everything to begin with. We pay taxes not because the government says we must pay taxes but because Jesus says we must pay taxes. And Jesus says we must pay taxes because, as Paul writes,

> The authorities that exist have been established by God.

This is the beginning of what it means to be subject to governing authorities. So does this mean we have to be subject to unjust and ungodly laws? No, it does not; however, should we choose to disobey such laws, we must be subject to the penalties and punishments imposed by the government (remember Shadrach, Meshach, and Abednego and a million martyrs in their wake).

To say "Jesus is Lord" explicitly implies Caesar is not Lord. Now, just because Caesar is not Lord does not mean Caesar does not have a significant role and responsibility. God has given Caesar, and any other government for that matter, whatever power and authority it holds. These authorities aren't merely subject to God, but they must also obey God. And they disobey at their peril, for they will answer to God. This is not our primary concern. Our concern is that we, too, will answer to God.

In closing, I repeat: Romans 13 is not meant to be a treatise on church-state relations. Paul is not going there. And neither am I. You already know that entire matter is a minefield. Let's not blow ourselves up, okay? Let's just pay our taxes and keep the peace. We have a much larger job to do than any government can conceive of. We are sowing a kingdom!

The Prayer

Abba Father! We understand the need for government and even that it is instituted by God, and yet we struggle mightily with bad government. We struggle profoundly to submit to bad and especially wicked government. And yet we confess that what we see as bad government bears no comparison to what those first Christians endured. We begin with this: Jesus is Lord, not the government nor the governors. In Jesus's name, we will submit to them, by the power of the Holy Spirit. We trust you, Father. We need wisdom, counsel, restraint, and supernatural guidance. Praying in Jesus's name. Amen.

The Questions

How do you understand these teachings of Paul and Jesus in our contemporary context? Where do you struggle with them? Do you see the potential pitfalls of the church being in league with the government?

Romans 13:4–5

69 | On Jesus, His Church, and the Government

> *For the one in authority is God's servant for your good. But if you do wrong, be afraid, for rulers do not bear the sword for no reason. They are God's servants, agents of wrath to bring punishment on the wrongdoer. Therefore, it is necessary to submit to the authorities, not only because of possible punishment but also as a matter of conscience.*

Consider This

Today's text should convince us that while Nero may have been the emperor of the day, he had not yet delved into the insanity he would be remembered for. How do we know that? Because it is hard to imagine Paul would write this about *that* Nero.

> For the one in authority is God's servant for your good.

Now that we have that settled, let's also be clear that Rome was not a friendly government. Rome was an equal opportunity oppressor, especially to Christians. The declaration "Jesus is Lord" would have been heard as a decisively political statement and interpreted as insurrectionist at best. While I indicated that Paul did not give us a treatise on church and government/state relations, he did give us clear theological thinking on the matter.

To say "Jesus is Lord" does not mean Jesus is in the state and government business. It does mean he is in authority over the business of government and state. Take a look at how Paul puts it in Ephesians:

> That power is the same as the mighty strength he exerted when he raised Christ from the dead and seated him at his right hand in the heavenly realms, far above all rule and authority, power and dominion, and every name that is invoked, not only in the present age but also in the one to come. And God placed all things under his feet and appointed him to be head over everything for the church, which is his body, the fullness of him who fills everything in every way. (Ephesians 1:19–23)

Notice the precise wording. It does not say God appointed the church to be head over everything for Jesus. No, it says something quite different, even opposite:

> God placed all things under his feet and appointed him to be head over everything for the church.

Jesus is Lord means he is the head of the church and he is the authority over the government. The great mistake repeatedly made through the centuries is the ill-fated leap to installing the church as the authority over the government and to do it in Jesus's name. The effect of this is to create a national church. It is a very short step from there to the effort to nationalize the Christian faith through the mechanisms of the government. While this is an ever-present seduction both for Christian politicians and despotic demagogues, it always results in disaster for the church, the government, and especially the people.

Now, it is a long way from ancient Rome to modern America, but there is a fascinating connective subtext as relates to the matters at hand. One truly brilliant stroke of genius by the founders of the United States was the establishment clause in the Constitution. It is in the first amendment of what we know as the Bill of Rights.

> Congress shall make no law respecting an establishment of religion, or prohibiting the free exercise thereof.

These are the first words of the first amendment (before free speech, free press, peaceable assembly, and petitioning the government with grievances). I believe those words reveal something about the theological mind of the founders—at least those who were Christians. They did not set out to create a Christian nation as much as they attempted to create a nation where people could freely be Christians, unhindered by the government. I have some experience and some learning on these matters, but I am not an expert. With my limited experience and understanding (and at the risk of gross oversimplification), here is what I believe the Bible points to concerning the relationship between church and state and, hence, what I surmise was in the minds of the founders of the United States.

1. Jesus is Lord; which means
2. Jesus is the head of the church, and
3. Jesus is Lord over all earthly governments, but
4. The church is not the head of the government for Jesus.
5. Jesus is the head of the government for the church. (It is a separate reporting relationship.)
6. Christians can and must provide leadership in the government, but this is for the sake of righteous leadership, merciful laws, and just courts rather than religious indoctrination.
7. In other words, we do not need or want a "Christian government" any more than we would want an "Islamic government."

We do want Christians (as well as others) serving in government to the end of a merciful and just and virtuous society.
8. It is not the role of the government to create a Christian nation. It is the role of the government to create a nation in which people can freely become and faithfully live as Christians, or live otherwise according to the dictates of their own conscience. It is the role of the church to sow the gospel of Jesus and his kingdom across this land and every other until the final trumpet sounds and "the kingdom of the world has become the kingdom of our Lord and of his Messiah, and he will reign for ever and ever" (Revelation 11:15).

Again, this is complex and well beyond my pay grade to even comment on, but as a pastor who happens to be a citizen living in this particularly troubled American context, I consider it my duty to speak from the limited wisdom I possess, exercising both courage and restraint and, yes, preparing for a beating. ;0)

The Prayer

Abba Father! It gives us great pleasure and is our deepest privilege to declare, Jesus is Lord! Forgive us for trying to impose Jesus on the world around us through the structures and strictures of the government. Holy Spirit, teach us and train us on our humble yet sacred place and role as your church in this world. "Grant us wisdom, grant us courage, for the facing of this hour."[3] Praying in Jesus's name. Amen.

The Questions

How are you challenged by the ideas in today's entry? Do you find yourself resonating or objecting? Say more. What is your theory on the case?

---

3. Harry Emerson Fosdick, "God of Grace and God of Glory," 1930.

Week 10: Discussion Questions

Hearing the Text

Read Romans 11:33–13:5.

Responding to the Text

- What did you hear?
- What did you see?
- What did you otherwise sense from the Lord?

Sharing Insights and Implications for Discipleship

Drawing from the Scripture text and daily readings, what did you find challenging, encouraging, provocative, comforting, invasive, inspiring, corrective, affirming, guiding, or warning?

Shaping Intentions for Prayer

Write your discipleship intention for the week ahead.

11
WEEK

Romans 13:6–14:12

Romans 13:6-7

71 — On Theology and Taxes

> This is also why you pay taxes, for the authorities are God's servants, who give their full time to governing. Give to everyone what you owe them: If you owe taxes, pay taxes; if revenue, then revenue; if respect, then respect; if honor, then honor.

Consider This

Let's wrap up our little experiment in crafting a working theology of government, taxes, Jesus, church, partisan politics, and dual citizenship.

I know. Some of you are thinking, "I might rather have my wisdom teeth extracted again today than this." Bear with me. This is every bit as spiritual as offering your body as a living sacrifice. Remember, to claim "Jesus is Lord" is to acknowledge that nothing falls outside his merciful and just jurisdiction. What follows is a combination of manifesto and commentary. So let's begin.

Paying taxes is a spiritual act of obedience to the God and Father of our Lord Jesus Christ. That said, I do hate paying taxes.

1. Jesus is Lord.
2. Government is necessary.

The purpose of government, at a bare minimum, is to protect people from one another (including protecting them from the government itself as well as from the governments and citizens of other sovereign lands). The preamble of the United States Constitution is a brilliant summative example of what a government constituted "under God" should aspire to. I include it here to illustrate:

> We the People of the United States, in Order to form a more perfect Union, establish Justice, insure domestic Tranquility, provide for the common defense, promote the general Welfare,

and secure the Blessings of Liberty to ourselves and our Posterity, do ordain and establish this Constitution for the United States of America.

Many among you of my generation can't read that without hearing the *Schoolhouse Rock!* tune to which we sang this preamble every Saturday morning during the cartoon hours of our childhood (look it up on YouTube). To my fellow Americans and readers, America has its problems, but these fifty-two words—with their five stated purposes—hammered out during the hot summer of 1787 hold its brilliance. It is truly a marvel.

3. Taxes are meant to fund the government.

> This is also why you pay taxes, for the authorities are God's servants, who give their full time to governing.

4. Notice that government authorities are God's servants, not by virtue of their being followers of God (which they may or may not be) but by virtue of Jesus being Lord over all governments. All governments are working under a delegation of authority from God, which means they are ultimately accountable to God. Their accountability to God will ultimately be measured by how they served the people, which makes a constitutional republic perhaps the best form of government invented to date. Why? Because, in the words of Abraham Lincoln, it is a government of the people, by the people, for the people. It avoids the concentration of power.

5. Note also when Paul says, "the authorities are God's servants," he is stating a fact, whether or not the authorities know this and whether or not they are acting as such. We think of governmental authorities (at least in the American context) as being accountable to the people. This may be true in a temporal fashion, but their line of accountability actually goes much higher. To the extent governmental authorities understand their accountabilities to God, they will better serve the people.

Now, I don't like to pay taxes. And honestly, I try to avoid paying taxes as much as possible under the law. (I would rather give my money to the church and directly to others in need.) I don't like the IRS. I often disagree with how my taxes are being spent. I often seriously think my taxes are being spent in ways that contravene the will and ways of God. And I live in America. How much more difficult must it have been for the Christians in first-century Rome with its tyrannical leaders? Yet Paul told them and us today to submit to the governing authorities and pay taxes.

I can't believe I am saying this, but if my logic holds (and it may not), paying taxes to the government is an act of faithfulness to God. I find myself on the brink of repentance. It's not that I think I'm going to all of a sudden be glad about paying taxes. I don't think that's the point. The point is about submitting to the government and its authorities in obedience to God.

Might there come a time when submission to the government means defiance of God? Yes. What then? Can we cross that bridge if and when we get there? I will say this by way of warning. The most important question at that juncture will be, "What does obedience to God require of us?" Many will jump to this question: "What shall be the manner of our defiance of the government?" The real (and frankly only) question must be: "What shall be the manner of our obedience to God?" As you are already noting, those are very, very different questions, and they will lead to very, very different responses and outcomes (see Romans 12).

The Prayer

Abba Father! Have mercy on us sinners, and by the grace of Jesus Christ make us true saints. We want the mind of Christ in every aspect of our lives: personally, as a church, and as citizens of the kingdom of heaven who are also living as citizens of nations and states on this earth. We pray for our nations and their governments and leaders, for wisdom and courage, for conviction and restraint. At the same time teach us what it means to love our enemies and to pray for those who persecute us. And come, Lord Jesus, come! Praying in Jesus's name. Amen.

The Questions

What is your response and reaction to these thoughts today? What wisdom is God giving you on these matters of everyday concern? How might we live out our primary citizenship as citizens of the kingdom of Jesus?

Romans 13:8–10

72 The Problem with Speed Limits and the Problem with Me

> Let no debt remain outstanding, except the continuing debt to love one another, for whoever loves others has fulfilled the law. The commandments, "You shall not commit adultery," "You shall not murder," "You shall not steal," "You shall not covet," and whatever other command there may be, are summed up in this one command: "Love your neighbor as yourself." Love does no harm to a neighbor. Therefore love is the fulfillment of the law.

Consider This

Does today's text feel like a hard left turn or, worse, like whiplash? I think so.

We go from submitting to the government and paying taxes to all of a sudden talking about love. This is one of those places where the chapter break (which is not part of the inspired text) throws us off. We tend to think new chapter, new subject, but the chapter break actually interrupts Paul's ongoing flow of thought. He's talking about love for the whole of chapter 12, and then he turns to one of the difficult test cases for love—the dad-gummed government.

Paul says submitting to the government by paying taxes is not ultimately about your compliance with the government for your own sake. It is about living for the sake of the greater good. Paying taxes is not about you. It's about other people. And it's about God. Here, Paul is pulling the thread of love back around.

> Let no debt remain outstanding, except the continuing debt to love one another, for whoever loves others has fulfilled the law.

For the longest time, I thought I obeyed the rules. I obeyed them as long as people were looking, but left to myself, much of the time all bets were off. You see, I had a self-focused orientation with laws and rules. Take the speed limit as an example.

Growing up, I would obey the speed limit if (a) my parents were in the car or (b) there was a police officer in the vicinity. Otherwise, I drove as fast as I could without feeling like I was endangering myself. In other words, I assumed the law was there for my good, and because I knew I was an exceptional driver, I believed I could go faster without hurting myself. So no harm no foul, right?

Wrong! In retrospect, it never occurred to me that the speed limit laws were primarily about other people. The law was designed to protect other people from me and me from other people. After all, driving involves piloting a four-thousand-pound hunk of metal. The point? I had a self-focused perspective on the law. It never once dawned on me that it was for the sake of other people and the good of the larger order.

I obeyed the law to the extent that my interest was served, which included (a) compliance in front of the right people to maintain my reputation while (b) getting where I wanted to go as quickly as possible. This is both self-interest and self-righteousness. The problem here is not with the law, it is with me. My fallen nature is to protect my self-interest while projecting my self-righteousness. Others do not come into that equation unless my aim is to deceive them. This is the deep, dark, and dastardly nature of Sin.

The gospel changes our nature from Sin (i.e., self-interested self-righteousness) to love (i.e., others-interested relational righteousness).

> Let no debt remain outstanding, except the continuing debt to love one another, for whoever loves others has fulfilled the law.

The purpose of the law is love. It is about God and other people.

> The commandments, "You shall not commit adultery," "You shall not murder," "You shall not steal," "You shall not covet," and whatever other command there may be [you shall not speed], are summed up in this one command: "Love your neighbor as yourself."

The goal of life and the will of God is to become the love of God, which requires consecration (i.e., in view of God's mercy to offer our bodies as a living sacrifice; Romans 12:1) leading to transformation (i.e., which is what happens when we conform not to the pattern of this world but are transformed by the renewing of our minds; Romans 12:2).

> Love does no harm to a neighbor. Therefore love is the fulfillment of the law.

Rather than a left turn or, worse, whiplash, Paul put his foot on the accelerator, moving us more and more into love, where he was going all the while.

The Prayer

Abba Father! Teach us to love until we have become love. We confess we are sinners, and yet we profess faith that we are becoming saints. Holy Spirit, would you fill us to overflowing with the love of God? Would you transform us by the renewing of our minds such that our love is not a fake self-interested self-righteous sham? Give us understanding such that our old perspective is undone and we begin to see everything through the lens of love—the blessing of neighbor and the good of the other. In other words, let Jesus be our vision. Praying in Jesus's name. Amen.

The Questions

Is your perspective on all this shifting? Are you seeing how love is the fulfillment of the Law and how if you have real love you don't need to even worry about the Law because you are not only obeying it but exceeding it?

73 | Romans 13:11–14
Stop Hitting the Snooze Bar!

> And do this, understanding the present time: The hour has already come for you to wake up from your slumber, because our salvation is nearer now than when we first believed. The night is nearly over; the day is almost here. So let us put aside the deeds of darkness and put on the armor of light. Let us behave decently, as in the daytime, not in carousing and drunkenness, not in sexual immorality and debauchery, not in dissension and jealousy. Rather, clothe yourselves with the Lord Jesus Christ, and do not think about how to gratify the desires of the flesh.

=== **Consider This** ===

On my phone, and probably yours too, among a thousand and one other features, there is an alarm clock. When the alarm goes off, a screen appears with several bits of information. At the top is the date. Below that is the time. Further down is the word *Alarm*. At the very bottom is a small grayish button with the word *Stop*. But just beneath the word *Alarm* and well above the button that says *Stop* is a large, oval-shaped, bright orange button. You know what it says: SNOOZE.

Pushing that button gets you nine more minutes of slumber. Why nine minutes? The reason dates back to the early digital alarm clocks, but sleep science offers a deeper logic. Somewhere between nine and twelve minutes our bodies begin the shift into a deep sleep cycle again. Nine minutes is the magic number to keep you from either fully waking up or fully going back to sleep. I read a study once saying that every time someone hits the snooze button, they forfeit 10 percent of their energy for the day. (I hear some of you doing the math out there with sighs of new understanding as to why you feel so sluggish today.)

As Paul turns toward the final stretch of Romans, he fires warning shots to the fledgling church in Rome. Today's text is a cannonball shot over the bow.

> And do this, understanding the present time: The hour has already come for you to wake up your slumber.

Of course, this is beautifully reminiscent of one of our other favorite words from Paul, which even in those early decades had already become a saying across the church:

This is why it is said:

> "Wake up, sleeper,
>   rise from the dead,
>   and Christ will shine on you." (Ephesians 5:14)

You see, Paul's audience is not the unbelieving world. He writes to the followers of Jesus. He is talking to awakened believers who have drifted into the nether land between sleep and wakefulness. And he is talking to the multitudes of us who have developed the bad habit of hitting snooze.

> The night is nearly over; the day is almost here.

The night has been defeated, and yet the darkness lingers as we await the dawn. Paul doesn't say, "Get out of bed," but rather "Rise from the dead." The ancient grip of death has been broken, but the human spirit is weak and often reticent to respond. The graveclothes of death—into which we are born—must be stripped away. Early belief must be met with patterned beholding if we are to move into the territory of real becoming. The "pattern[s] of this world" do not let go easily. To "be transformed by the renewing of your mind" (Romans 12:2) takes more than just setting an alarm clock paired with good intentions.

Some years ago I picked up a collection of poems by Tom Hennen based on the title alone: *Darkness Sticks to Everything*. Darkness, like death, has been destroyed by the death and resurrection of Jesus Christ, and yet it is true—darkness still sticks to everything. Hear Paul out:

> So let us put aside the deeds of darkness and put on the armor of light.

This is not a motivational pep talk to live by better principles. Paul knows that all around us there is a war raging against our souls. He knows we will need a different kind of armor altogether—the armor of light. Wow! What a picture!

> Let us behave decently, as in the daytime, not in carousing and drunkenness, not in sexual immorality and debauchery, not in dissension and jealousy.

Putting aside the deeds of darkness does not mean simply trying harder to be better. Paul is not advocating for a life filled with better principles and platitudes. Jesus is not after a "principled life." It turns out, those people are the worst snooze-bar offenders of all, deceiving themselves by their principles while hiding behind their self-interested and self-righteous image management.

The "principled life" parades as light but remains deceptively cloaked in darkness. I know that stings for some of you. You will thank me later. Abandon the pretense of a "principled life" with all its reasonable respectability. You were an abject, brazen sinner not so long ago. You are slowly slipping back into the "desires of the flesh." Stop deceiving yourselves with a religion-wrapped life. Your principles, even godly religious ones, will not save you. They are powerless against the wiles of sin.

> Rather, clothe yourselves with the Lord Jesus Christ.

The remedy: Throw away the entire wardrobe of image management. Put on the identity of Jesus Christ by the indwelling Holy Spirit.

The armor of light is the indwelling Jesus Christ, who wears the vestments of holy love, donning them in the deepest places of our inmost selves and lives. Only Jesus produces the radiance we long for. The way is consecration, transformation, and demonstration.

Can we commit to each other—no more snooze bar?

Wake up, sleeper, rise from the dead, and Christ will shine on you!

The Prayer

Abba Father! We don't know what we don't know, especially about ourselves. And thinking we are on the right path does not mean we are on the right path. We are so prone—nay, I am so prone—to hit the snooze button in my life with Jesus. I slowly and seductively forget just how desperate I am for his presence in my life. Train me in what it means to clothe myself with the Lord Jesus Christ (Romans 13:14). I want this wardrobe, recognizing these are not outer garments nor shiny regalia but the inner vestments of holy love. Have mercy on me, a sinner becoming a saint. Praying in Jesus's name. Amen.

The Questions

Do you see your own propensity to hit the snooze button on your life and faith in Jesus? Will you pray for the Holy Spirit to pierce the veil of any self-deception in you? Are you willing to become brazenly honest about what he shows you?

Romans 14:1–4

74 Sweat the Small Stuff— and It's All Small Stuff

> *Accept the one whose faith is weak, without quarreling over disputable matters. One person's faith allows them to eat anything, but another, whose faith is weak, eats only vegetables. The one who eats everything must not treat with contempt the one who does not, and the one who*

> does not eat everything must not judge the one who does, for God has accepted them. Who are you to judge someone else's servant? To their own master, servants stand or fall. And they will stand, for the Lord is able to make them stand.

Consider This

These Roman followers of Jesus were waiting for chapter 14. They would have listened carefully to each of the prior thirteen chapters, looking for clues as to how Paul was going to deal with their $64,000 question: How is Paul going to deal with our big problems?

What would Paul say about eating meat, drinking wine, and keeping Sabbath laws? Disagreement was tearing the community apart, and they couldn't come to any peace around it. They had arrived at the place of irreconcilable convictions.

In one corner were the Jews (best we can tell). They brought with them the Law and all its requirements of circumcision, dietary restrictions, and the observance of the Sabbath.

In the other corner were the gentiles. They were the newcomers to the faith. They had no problem with food and drink—meat and wine—and they weren't about to be circumcised and keep Sabbath.

The Jews would have been regarded as the "weaker" in faith because they couldn't abide letting go of their Jewishness with all the rites, rituals, and culture. In fact, they expected the gentiles (i.e., the stronger ones) to adopt their customs as a matter of requirement. The gentiles weren't having it. They knew they didn't have to become Jews to follow Jesus. And they looked down on the Jews because they would not let go of the old in order to live in the new covenant.

The Jews were struggling to keep fellowship with the gentiles because of this and took great offense at the brazen insensibility of their ways. Each group likely considered the other infidels.

This is the big brouhaha in the little church of a hundred in the midst of the million lost souls in Rome. This is why Paul wrote the letter to begin with. This hostile dispute is the pretext and subtext and the real reason we have this most famous letter ever written.

You've heard the saying "Don't sweat the small stuff. And it's all small stuff." It's not true. This is a story of how the little things turn out to be the big things.

For Paul, the big picture of winning Rome came down to this tiny community and their relationships. Could they, in their relationships with each other, witness to the reconciliation of the gospel in Jesus Christ? Everything, in a sense, was on the line.

That's on the docket for this week, wrestling through the small things that turn out to be the big things in Jesus's name. It may even lead us to see the same trends and troubles in our own day and age.

We will see, in the end, that it's not really about meat and wine and Sabbath at all but about their relationships and the love of Jesus unleashed therein. We are going to see the righteousness of God unveiled and revealed in the most important mission field of all: our relationships inside the church. We will discover the secret sauce of the whole project.

Our relationships are the mission.

The Prayer

Abba Father! Thank you that the small things matter when it comes to following Jesus and his royal way of loving God and neighbor. Prepare us for deeper understanding of what matters most. Awaken us to the way the small things are the big things when it comes to the gospel and our relationships with each other in the church. Prepare us for the deep revelation now coming to a climax in this letter. Praying in Jesus's name. Amen.

The Questions

How does this notion strike you: Our relationships are the mission? Does it resonate? Do you have pushback?

Romans 14:5–9

75

When the Conflict Is Not About the Conflict and What It Is Really About

> One person considers one day more sacred than another; another considers every day alike. Each of them should be fully convinced in their own mind. Whoever regards one day as special does so to the Lord. Whoever eats meat does so to the Lord, for they give thanks to God; and whoever abstains does so to the Lord and gives thanks to God. For none of us lives for ourselves alone, and none of us dies for ourselves alone. If we live, we live for the Lord; and if we die, we die for the Lord. So, whether we live or die, we belong to the Lord. For this very reason, Christ died and returned to life so that he might be the Lord of both the dead and the living.

Consider This

What do people living in Christian community do when they come to a disputed matter and it breaks down into an irreconcilable conflict?

They get out their Bibles, stake out the high ground, and play the God card, of course! That wasn't exactly the case with the Roman Christians, yet it was close. We all tend to appeal to a higher authority in order to win the day.

In today's text, we have the Jewish argument for Sabbath-keeping and the gentile case against it. Now watch Paul the Jew weigh in:

> One person considers one day more sacred than another; another considers every day alike.

Paul wants them to be clear about the conviction on which they stand. Paul is not calling for anyone to compromise their convictions. He is not looking for some kind of mushy middle compromise from people whose convictions are in conflict. He says,

> Each of them should be fully convinced in their own mind.

Paul does not make the mistake that many in our time make, which is to try to devise political solutions to theological conflicts that require untenable compromises against conscience. Rather, he does the opposite, leading us to think theologically about political conflicts.

To do this, Paul doesn't begin by trying to bring the parties together. No, he calls them to stand with their conviction before God.

Watch his masterful approach:

> Whoever regards one day as special does so to the Lord. Whoever eats meat does so to the Lord, for they give thanks to God; and whoever abstains does so to the Lord and gives thanks to God.

Paul shifts the issue from a dispute between fractured parties to a matter of one's personal relationship with and devotion to the Lord Jesus. The message: It is God with whom you have to deal. In doing this he honors their competing convictions, defusing their division by calling them to stand before God, in whom is found the higher ground of their unity.

> For none of us lives for ourselves alone, and none of us dies for ourselves alone. If we live, we live for the Lord; and if we die, we die for the Lord. So, whether we live or die, we belong to the Lord.

When we find ourselves in irreconcilable conflict over matters of conscience and convictions, we aren't apt to work them out directly with each other. We must come before God, who alone can sift and sort our hearts and minds. We must come to a place beyond ourselves where we can recover our sense of what personal Lordship means. You saw it right there in the text:

> If we live, we live for the Lord; and if we die, we die for the Lord. So, whether we live or die, we belong to the Lord.

We each must personally come to the place of refreshing our consecration. We must realize that we are not our own. That we have been bought with a price. That there are great purposes and designs for our lives, which are most fully realized in and through our relationships with each other.

Behold! In a Holy Spirit–inspired masterstroke of divine genius, Paul takes us to the cross.

> For this very reason, Christ died and returned to life so that he might be the Lord of both the dead and the living.

When conflict is high and solutions are low, it is only from this holiest of level ground that we can hope to really find each other again.

And this, my friends, is why the letter doesn't begin with chapter 14. We need the full panoramic view of God's mercy first.

The Prayer

Abba Father! We have the sense that our deepest conflicts are not about our conflicts but rather about the deep brokenness in our lives. We've all been broken in and through our relationships, and unhealed, we break others in relationships. We need the healing of the cross. We need our salvation to grow well beyond a transaction of pardon and into the deeper mercies of transforming grace. Lift us out of our conflicted and broken relationships and into your loving presence. Heal us to the depths. Fit us for relationships with others by forming us in our relationship with you. Holy Spirit, restore us to belovedness that we might become beacons and bearers of belovedness to others—where in embrace we forget even what we were fighting about. Praying in Jesus's name. Amen.

The Questions

What are you noticing about Paul's theological wisdom and his pastoral skill? Have you realized that the conflict in your relationships is not really about the conflict but about the brokenness of the parties?

Romans 14:10–12

76

The Four Horsemen of the Apocalypse

> *You, then, why do you judge your brother or sister? Or why do you treat them with contempt? For we will all stand before God's judgment seat. It is written:*
>
> > *"'As surely as I live,' says the Lord,*
> > *'every knee will bow before me;*
> > *every tongue will acknowledge God.'"*
>
> *So then, each of us will give an account of ourselves to God.*

=== **Consider This** ===

Let's rehearse the story so far on Romans 14.

1. Paul acknowledges the conflict and deems it a nonessential matter.
2. He shifts the conflict from warring factions to personalized reckoning.
3. He asks them to personally clarify their convictions.
4. Rather than bringing them face-to-face into some kind of mediated conflict resolution, he pushes them to deal personally and directly with God.
5. Now, in today's text, ten verses in, he identifies the real issue and calls them out.

> You, then, why do you judge your brother or sister?

The issues here are eating meat, drinking wine, and keeping Sabbath. The underlying matter is of another order entirely. It is the soul cancer of judgment and judging one another. Paul knows nothing will destroy this little church faster than the spirit of judgment among the people. He also knows where this leads.

> Or why do you treat them with contempt?

If the spirit of judgment constitutes the cancerous cells, then the sign of their malignant spread is contempt. Paul chooses a strong word here: *exoutheneó*. It goes way past judging others and into the realm of mockery and despising them.

Some years ago, the celebrated Jewish psychologist John Gottman embarked on a landmark research study on divorce and its causes. He developed a model that could predict eventual divorce with a documented 90 percent accuracy rate based on the presence of certain behavioral markers. Through his research, he identified four relational cascading markers that point to and ultimately cause relational dissolution. They occur progressively and in this order: criticism, defensiveness, contempt, and stonewalling. He called them "The Four Horsemen of the Apocalypse."

Take note, modern readers—especially those of us dealing with church conflicts (not to mention marital and other relational impasses)—of Paul's prescription. Before we need an exploration of the conflict, we need an examination of conscience before God.[1] So often we try to resolve conflict with others before we have dealt with ourselves in the presence of God. It invariably results in escalating the conflict. This is so because most of our conflicts reach an impasse because of our own deep investment in being right.

> For we will all stand before God's judgment seat. It is written:

---

1. If I were a marriage counselor (and I'm not), I would develop an examination of conscience, and I think I would begin the whole process by separately leading both the husband and the wife through this examination in the presence of God. I think I would instruct them to engage in this process every day for a week or two before we even began the process. I am learning from Paul that until people in a relationship are actually dealing personally with God there is really no point in trying to resolve complex relational conflicts between them. I say this also in the spirit of Jesus's words concerning judging others and on removing the log from one's own eye before trying to take the speck out of someone else's eye.

> "'As surely as I live,' says the Lord,
> 'every knee will bow before me;
> every tongue will acknowledge God.'"

Translation: Do not pass go. Do not collect $200. Go straight to the throne of God. Run to the foot of the cross. Bow and kneel at the feet of Jesus. Declare with your mouth, "Jesus Christ is Lord." Refresh the faith of your heart that God raised him from the dead. Invite the Holy Spirit to lay bare your heart and search you and grant you a spirit of repentance. Repent of a judgmental spirit, of criticism, of defensiveness, of contempt, and of stonewalling.

So then, each of us will give an account of ourselves to God.

Paul invites the followers of Jesus, then and now, to go ahead and get in the habit of giving this account to God, who alone is the Judge—while there is still time to recover and make amends. This is the great miracle of mercy and the mystery of grace.

The Prayer

Abba Father! Thank you that you are the righteous Judge. Forgive us when we attempt to usurp your authority by inserting ourselves in your place. We confess we get crossways with other people and escalate our conflicts when we fail to find ourselves alone at the cross before you. You are the Judge, and we can entrust ourselves to you who judges justly, just as Jesus did. Holy Spirit, would you teach us this way of turning away from the escalating conflict and turning directly to you? This is wisdom, and for it we thank you. Praying in Jesus's name. Amen.

The Questions

Do you find yourself embroiled in conflicted relationships where things have turned judgmental and contemptuous? Are you motivated to find yourself at the feet of Jesus to wrestle this out?

Week 11: Discussion Questions

Hearing the Text

Read Romans 13:6–14:12.

Responding to the Text

- What did you hear?
- What did you see?
- What did you otherwise sense from the Lord?

Sharing Insights and Implications for Discipleship

Drawing from the Scripture text and daily readings, what did you find challenging, encouraging, provocative, comforting, invasive, inspiring, corrective, affirming, guiding, or warning?

Shaping Intentions for Prayer

Write your discipleship intention for the week ahead.

Week 11:
Discussion Questions

Hearing the Text
Read Romans 1:16–17:25.

Responding to the Text
* What did you hear?
* What did you notice?
* What did you draw/sense from the text?

Sharing Insights and Implications for Discipleship
Drawing from the insights and understandings gained, what did you find challenging, encouraging, informative, comforting, inspiring, learning connections with the readings? (optional)

Shaping Intercessions for Prayer
Write your own discussion questions for the week ahead.

12
WEEK

Romans 14:13–15:22

Romans 14:13-18

78 Sometimes When You Are Right You Are Wrong

> *Therefore let us stop passing judgment on one another. Instead, make up your mind not to put any stumbling block or obstacle in the way of a brother or sister. I am convinced, being fully persuaded in the Lord Jesus, that nothing is unclean in itself. But if anyone regards something as unclean, then for that person it is unclean. If your brother or sister is distressed because of what you eat, you are no longer acting in love. Do not by your eating destroy someone for whom Christ died. Therefore do not let what you know is good be spoken of as evil. For the kingdom of God is not a matter of eating and drinking, but of righteousness, peace and joy in the Holy Spirit, because anyone who serves Christ in this way is pleasing to God and receives human approval.*

Consider This

There is a saying that has circulated around the church since at least the time of Augustine. The saying has been attributed to many theologians, including John Wesley, and is widely accepted as wisdom. Here it is:

In essentials, unity; in nonessentials, liberty; in all things, charity.

The hard part, and where significant disagreement arises, comes in sorting out what is essential and what is nonessential. Paul seems to say that the matter of eating meat and drinking wine is a nonessential matter. In other words, there is room for people to adopt divergent positions. He goes further to say that no food is unclean. In nonessentials, liberty. End of discussion.

Not so fast. Just because people have the freedom to follow their own conscience here does not mean the conversation is over. It simply means the doctrinal issue has been adjudicated. The laws around eating and drinking under the old covenant are no longer applicable. It raises the last phrase in the famous saying: In all things, charity. Does my exercising my freedom cause harm to you? Is my freedom being exercised in love for others, or is it centered on myself and my own interests?

> If your brother or sister is distressed because of what you eat, you are no longer acting in love. Do not by your eating destroy someone for whom Christ died.

Paul calls the church to wake up and realize they are now kneeling at the foot of the cross together. He rebuked them for judging one another. Now he calls them to love one another. Can we recognize our common frailty as broken human beings? Can I realize Jesus died for me and also for you? If me exercising my freedom causes you to stumble, is it worth it to persist in exercising my freedom? No. Sometimes the exercising of my own rights can be wrong. In these times, the right thing to do is to sacrifice my right for the sake of my brother or sister. Sometimes the exercise of non-sinful freedom can become sinful. The question is not whether it is legal but whether it is loving. It falls under the rubric, Sometimes when you are right, you are wrong.

While the consumption of certain ceremonial foods is not a significant issue for most Christians today, Paul's point can be applied to the topic of alcohol consumption. Although the rationale has evolved since the first century, the core message remains relevant. Given the widespread issue of alcohol addiction both within and outside the church, and the fact that drinking can be a stumbling block for many, it is a discussion worth having.

Bottom line:

> Instead, make up your mind not to put any stumbling block or obstacle in the way of a brother or sister.

The Prayer

Abba Father! I confess that sometimes I get so wrapped up in whether something is right or wrong, I can easily fall into judging those I disagree with. Other times I get so caught up in my own rights that I can be wrong in the way

I stand on them. I ask you to forgive me for these sins and yet, more than that, to transform me such that love for others becomes not just my core conviction but my deepest nature. Save me from fooling myself into believing I can be all about Jesus without being all about other people. Holy Spirit, train my inmost being to love as Jesus loves. Praying in Jesus's name. Amen.

The Questions

Are you grasping that real righteousness is not about being right but about our relationships—with God and others? Are you learning to hold your convictions in ways that are loving toward others and not judgmental, condemning, and ultimately sinful?

Romans 14:19–23

79 Yes, Our Relationships Are the Mission

> Let us therefore make every effort to do what leads to peace and to mutual edification. Do not destroy the work of God for the sake of food. All food is clean, but it is wrong for a person to eat anything that causes someone else to stumble. It is better not to eat meat or drink wine or to do anything else that will cause your brother or sister to fall.
>
> So whatever you believe about these things keep between yourself and God. Blessed is the one who does not condemn himself by what he approves. But whoever has doubts is condemned if they eat, because their eating is not from faith; and everything that does not come from faith is sin.

Consider This

I began the conversation on Romans 14 with this bold declaration: Our relationships are the mission. I say this based on my reading of the whole Bible, most notably the New Testament, and particularly these words of our Lord Jesus Christ:

> My prayer is not for them alone. I pray also for those who will believe in me through their message, that all of them may be one, Father, just as you are in me and I am in you. May they also be in us so that the world may believe that you have sent me. (John 17:20–21)

Jesus prayed for two things: (1) for us to be in relationship with each other in the same way he and the Father are in relationship with each other (in the fellowship of the Holy Spirit) and (2) for our relationships to be anchored in and animated by the relationship between the Father and the Son (in the fellowship of the Holy Spirit).

Why is this so important to Jesus? The faith of the unbelieving world depends on the relationships of the people within the believing church.

Hence my declaration: Our relationships are the mission.

But why? One word: *love*. The apostle John may have said it best: "God is love. Whoever lives in love lives in God, and God in them" (1 John 4:16). The most sovereign demonstration of the power of God is the love of God, and we need look no further than the cross. In the death and resurrection of Jesus Christ, we see the powerful, saving love of God on full display, issuing forth in the justice, mercy, grace, and peace of God. The church Jesus is building is an ever-unfolding iconic revelation of these divine realities through the relationships of the people enfolded therein. If what people see in our relationships is a denial of what they read in the Bible, we effectively give them a reason not to believe.

Hear Paul to the Ephesians on this point:

> As a prisoner for the Lord, then, I urge you to live a life worthy of the calling you have received. Be completely humble and gentle; be patient, bearing with one another in love. Make every effort to keep the unity of the Spirit through the bond of peace. (Ephesians 4:1–3)

The bond of peace is the strongest bond in the cosmos, and yet it is also quite fragile. It is as strong as the sovereign love of God, and yet it is as vulnerable as the brokenness of people. On the one hand, when it comes to the church Jesus is building, the gates of hell will not prevail against it, but when the followers of Jesus engage in permissible behavior that causes one another to stumble in their faith, it can create a crisis of New Testament proportions. In first-century Rome, it came down to what they were having for supper.

From the first century to the twenty-first century, relational conflict within the church is a given. That's not the issue. It all comes down to how we engage with one another in the midst of conflict. In many ways, the history of the church is a history of conflict. Sometimes, especially when it comes to nonessential matters, the conflicts can be worked out and communities can reconcile. At other times, when the issues are entwined with more essential concerns, reconciliation may not be possible. Reconciliation or not, the peace of Jesus Christ is always available in our relationships. And it is imperative we make every effort to avail ourselves of this costly peace. Remember, our relationships are the mission, regardless of the outcome. Peace can be made in the wake of the worst irreconcilable differences. Depart throwing roses, never rocks.

In the third stanza of the magisterial hymn "The Church's One Foundation," we have these words:

> Tho' with a scornful wonder,
> we see her sore oppressed,
> by schisms rent asunder,
> by heresies distressed,
> yet saints their watch are keeping,
> their cry goes up, "How long?"
> And soon the night of weeping
> shall be the morn of song.[1]

Let's be clear. Our broken relationships within the church grieve the Holy Spirit, and they may compromise the witness of Jesus through his church, but they neither disrupt nor disturb the unity of the triune

---

1. Samuel J. Stone, "The Church's One Foundation," 1866.

God. The God and Father of our Lord Jesus Christ plays the long game. He has waited out many a hard-hearted bishop, suffered both necessary and needless schisms, made allowance for zealous fools, tolerated obstinate men and women, endured misguided heretics and absurd heresies, and allowed centuries to pass, yet all the while his truth is marching on. He may seem to lose a battle here and there—and even on our watch—but he will win the war.

Indeed, he has already won.

The Prayer

Abba Father! Thank you for your son, Jesus, our Lord, who is the Prince of Peace. Keep us near the cross, day by day, hour by hour. Impress on us by your Spirit the importance of our relationships inside the church. Holy Spirit, would you fill us with the love of God for one another, the love that is full of mercy and grace, that gives the benefit of the doubt, that forgives and makes peace, even when it's hard? Too much is at stake. Make our relationships places of your revelation. Make our relationships places where your mission of winning the world is accomplished. Praying in Jesus's name. Amen.

The Questions

Are you understanding the point: Our relationships are the mission? Do you have any broken relationships with people in the body of Christ that need mending? Will you pray about the pathway to get there?

80 | Romans 15:1–4
Awakening Rides on the Rails of Friendship

> *We who are strong ought to bear with the failings of the weak and not to please ourselves. Each of us should please our neighbors for their good, to build them up. For even Christ did not please himself but,*

> as it is written: "The insults of those who insult you have fallen on
> me." For everything that was written in the past was written to teach
> us, so that through the endurance taught in the Scriptures and the
> encouragement they provide we might have hope.

Consider This

Last week I shared with you one of the core convictions of life in the kingdom of Jesus: Our relationships are the mission. I repeat this frequently with the Farm Team at Seedbed.

There is another saying we are fond of in our community: Awakening rides on the rails of friendship. If our relationships are the mission, it makes sense that our primary work is in building these bonds as strong as we can. Relationships that are broken and in disrepair create barriers not only for the flourishing of the church but for the awakening of the unbelieving world.

Though Paul's letters are filled with theological reflection and pastoral wisdom, we must remember his purpose in all of them was to build up the body of Christ. Much, if not most, of the time, this meant dealing with the brokenness in their relationships. I marvel at these words of Paul in his letter to the church at Philippi:

> I plead with Euodia and I plead with Syntyche to be of the same
> mind in the Lord. Yes, and I ask you, my true companion, help
> these women since they have contended at my side in the cause
> of the gospel. (Philippians 4:2–3)

How would you like to be Euodia and Syntyche, forever identified and called out as those two people who couldn't work out their conflict? We don't know why they were at odds, but their unresolved conflict, small as it likely was in the scheme of things, is forever a conflict of biblical proportions. Why? Because it was becoming a hindrance to the mission of this first little church in all of Europe. If awakening rides on the rails of friendship, then a broken friendship can derail the whole train.

And that's the point, isn't it? It's the small things. It is the unaddressed slight, the unspoken hurt, the passive-aggressive offense, or the untended hurt that leads to an unmended relationship.

> Each of us should please our neighbors for their good, to build them up.

Remember Paul's urgent exhortation to the little church in Ephesus: "Make every effort to keep the unity of the Spirit through the bond of peace" (Ephesians 4:3).

The whole reason Paul wrote this letter to the Romans was to try to rehabilitate their relationships, which were threatening to derail the awakening afoot in Rome. Could it be that the broken relationships in my life are creating a barrier to awakening in my community?

Have you ever considered that the broken, unhealed, and untended relationships in your life could do so much damage? Is it worth it to let them persist? This is not a word of condemnation; rather, it is a word of great hope. What if it could be that simple? (Note: I didn't say *easy*.) What if we began to mend the broken relationships in our communities? That would certainly lead to firstfruits of awakening in our midst.

The Prayer

Abba Father! We knew our relationships mattered to you, but we never really knew how much was riding on them. We are the body of Christ. Forgive us for thinking of it as a mere metaphor. We are actually part of each other, so is it any wonder that when our bonds with each other are broken the whole body suffers? Holy Spirit, awaken us to the gravity of this reality, not in condemnation but with fresh hope, realizing that our relationships mended and ever mending could lead to awakening in others, not to mention renewed love and joy in our own lives. We are willing. I am willing. Show me the next small step. Praying in Jesus's name. Amen.

The Questions

Do you have a Holy Spirit story about a broken relationship now mending or already mended? Are there broken relationships in your family, in your church, with people outside the church you long to see healed and mended? Will you bring these before Jesus?

81 | Romans 15:5–6
Unus Christianus, Nullus Christianus

> May the God who gives endurance and encouragement give you the same attitude of mind toward each other that Christ Jesus had, so that with one mind and one voice you may glorify the God and Father of our Lord Jesus Christ.

═══ Consider This ═══

There it is. I've never spotted it before.

> May the God who gives endurance and encouragement give you the same attitude of mind toward each other that Christ Jesus had.

It's like holy déjà vu. Paul said the same thing to the Philippian church (speaking of Euodia and Syntyche)!

> Let the same mind be in you that was in Christ Jesus. (Philippians 2:5 NRSVue)

Of course, this takes us back to the Jesus Manifesto in Romans 12:

> Do not conform to the pattern of this world, but be transformed by the renewing of your mind. (v. 2)

The Spirit transforms us by renewing our minds by giving us the mind of Jesus Christ. Here is the warning: We can only go so far in this process by ourselves. And "going to church" often is sadly just another way to remain quasi-anonymous in a crowd. To have "the same attitude of mind toward each other that Christ Jesus had" requires consecrated relationships. (Remember the path—consecration, transformation, demonstration). We must press past the comfortable anonymity of being in a crowd. We must go beyond the cozy connections of our "community groups" and smaller "life groups." These are good, and good things happen there, but the church today is largely missing the critical connection of microcommunities, what history calls "bands." *Band* is a word for a transformational microcommunity.[2]

The early church had a saying: *Unus Christianus, nullus Christianus.* Translation: One Christian, no Christian. Deciding to be baptized and follow Jesus is a personal decision. No one can do that for another person. However, to become a real Christian takes other Christians. Transformational faith is a team sport; it requires a lot of one-anothering. Hence, one Christian, no Christian.

Main street Christianity thinks transformation by the renewing of the mind comes through learning more information. Consequently, most of our groups are built around Bible studies and curricular resources. Again, those aren't bad, just inadequate for the real work of transformation. Maybe this is why our churches grow numerically but not in the transformational metrics of holiness described in the New Testament. Perhaps this is why we feel stuck in the same sin patterns and habits that have plagued us for years. We simply do not have the kind of relationships envisioned by the New Testament to sustain the kind of transformation needed to become who God made us to be and to do what God designed us to do.

What we need are smaller settings where our lives become the curriculum. That is the place where we realize we can become the trusted friends of Jesus only by becoming the trusted friends of a couple of others in Jesus's presence through the fellowship of the Holy Spirit. In this way, a band is different from a typical small group. And these types of gatherings/bands are where miracles like this happen:

---

2. Learn more about discipleship bands here: discipleshipbands.com.

> May the God who gives endurance and encouragement give you the same attitude of mind toward each other that Christ Jesus had, so that with one mind and one voice you may glorify the God and Father of our Lord Jesus Christ.

Endurance, encouragement, love, deep transformation, and the glory of God—these are what happen in a band. This is not advanced Christianity. A band is not just for people who have been around the church for a while. It is for everyone. If our relationships are the mission, as I believe they are, and if awakening rides on the rails of friendship, which I believe is so, then banding is among the most essential practices in the kingdom of Jesus.

Unus Christianus, nullus Christianus. One Christian, no Christian.

The Prayer

Abba Father! Thank you for Jesus, who is our endurance and encouragement in the Spirit. He is our glory and the lifter of our heads. Thank you for the way he can do this in us through a few others in the transforming grace of covenant love—in the bond of a band. Impress on us that while we tend to build our churches on crowds we call community, you build your church with the smallest bonds of love, with real friendship, showing us that if we can learn to truly love two or three others, we have learned to love the world. I confess, it is so easy to believe the opposite. Holy Spirit, lead me into this old new way. Praying in Jesus's name. Amen.

The Questions

Are you committed to gathering with a smaller group of people and making your lives the curriculum? If not, what's stopping you?

Romans 15:7–13

82

From Shepherding to Fishing

> *Accept one another, then, just as Christ accepted you, in order to bring praise to God. For I tell you that Christ has become a servant of the Jews on behalf of God's truth, so that the promises made to the patriarchs might be confirmed and, moreover, that the Gentiles might glorify God for his mercy. As it is written:*
>
> > *"Therefore I will praise you among the Gentiles;*
> > *I will sing the praises of your name."*
>
> *Again, it says,*
>
> > *"Rejoice, you Gentiles, with his people."*
>
> *And again,*
>
> > *"Praise the Lord, all you Gentiles;*
> > *let all the peoples extol him."*
>
> *And again, Isaiah says,*
>
> > *"The Root of Jesse will spring up,*
> > *one who will arise to rule over the nations;*
> > *in him the Gentiles will hope."*
>
> *May the God of hope fill you with all joy and peace as you trust in him, so that you may overflow with hope by the power of the Holy Spirit.*

Consider This

I believe the Old Testament could be called a sheep herding expedition. The primary exemplar is a shepherd. So what about the New Testament? I would call the New Testament a massive fishing expedition. But why did God call fishermen instead of shepherds? It is quite a change. I have wondered about this for years. I think I finally understand.

It's because in the shift from the Old Testament to the New Testament, God was not looking to add a lost sheep here and there. This shift from the old covenant to the new covenant meant the hope of adding to the community every non-Jewish person in the world. Today's text reveals yet again how God's plan is global in scope. It always has been. It took sending his Son to fulfill the plan. God's plan has always been to raise up a people—a community living in covenant relationship together with him, through whom he could reveal himself to the world and reconcile them in relationship.

> "Therefore I will praise you among the Gentiles;
> I will sing the praises of your name."

Again, it says,

> "Rejoice, you Gentiles, with his people."

And again,

> "Praise the Lord, all you Gentiles;
> let all the peoples extol him."

And again, Isaiah says,

> "The Root of Jesse will spring up,
> one who will arise to rule over the nations;
> in him the Gentiles will hope."

No, this is not adding a few stray sheep from the tribe of Judah. We are now talking about the whole world. Yes, this is a massive fishing expedition.

Growing up I had another misconception. When Jesus said his followers would be fishers of people, I immediately assumed he meant cane poles and rods and reels replete with live bait and artificial lures. Yes, I assumed he was talking about bait fishing. It turns out, New Testament fishing was all about net fishing.

Now, here's the kicker. In this massive New Testament fishing expedition, the people of God would become the net. But wait, you may ask, what is a net? It is quite simply a collection of knots. To continue this metaphor, the knots are our relationships. The knots aren't just any relationship, though, as if Facebook-friendship level would suffice. No, the knots are covenanted relationships. The knots are friendships in the tradition of the friends of Jesus. You knew I would get here. The knots are banded and bonded relationships, people learning to love one another with the very love of God.

Other people get caught up in the net when they are enfolded into our relationships, and in time they become knotted in. I believe the greatest biblical symbol of the New Testament church, the covenant community of Father, Son, and Holy Spirit, is the symbol we have largely overlooked: the net. When those first disciples responded to Jesus's call to follow him and become fishers of people, the Bible says they left their nets behind. Jesus would transform their lives and relationships into that net, and then he would throw them out like a net into the deep waters of the world.

It's time we picked up the net again as the sign and symbol both of the church and of our churches. The success of our churches will depend on the supernatural strength of our relationships therein. Are you seeing it? Our relationships are the mission. Awakening depends on the strength of the knots.

Paul wrote this letter to the Romans, those hundred or so Christians in the city of a million, to mend the net of their community. To re-band those disciples by retying the tattering knots.

The most important work ahead of us is learning to tie New Testament knots again. If "church" does not exist at the micro level, it does not exist at all. Truth be told, we have to relearn to net fish all over again because we have mistakenly spent the last hundred years or so perfecting the model of bait fishing. Bait fishing is trying to attract people to our churches with all manner of shiny things. Net fishing is about banding together and going out where the fish are, in the shallows and deeps of the real world.

The Prayer

Abba Father! Thank you for sending your Son to catch fish, and that he started with fishermen and women, and that he tied them together in the knot of his relationship with you in the fellowship of the Holy Spirit. Teach us how to tie such New Testament knots that become so unbreakable that others become caught up in the love we share. We pray for our churches to recover this netfishing mindset. Start with me. Start with my band. Start with tying a knot between me and a couple of others, for the world. Praying in Jesus's name. Amen.

The Questions

Are the eyes of your heart opening to the imagery and vision of the New Testament church as a net and how that net is the knots of our relationships? What are the implications of this idea?

Romans 15:14–22

83 | Ask Me About My Band

> I myself am convinced, my brothers and sisters, that you yourselves are full of goodness, filled with knowledge and competent to instruct one another. Yet I have written you quite boldly on some points to remind you of them again, because of the grace God gave me to be a minister of Christ Jesus to the Gentiles. He gave me the priestly duty of proclaiming the gospel of God, so that the Gentiles might become an offering acceptable to God, sanctified by the Holy Spirit.

> *Therefore I glory in Christ Jesus in my service to God. I will not venture to speak of anything except what Christ has accomplished through me in leading the Gentiles to obey God by what I have said and done—by the power of signs and wonders, through the power of the Spirit of God. So from Jerusalem all the way around to Illyricum, I have fully proclaimed the gospel of Christ. It has always been my ambition to preach the gospel where Christ was not known, so that I would not be building on someone else's foundation. Rather, as it is written:*
>
> > *"Those who were not told about him will see,*
> > *and those who have not heard will understand."*
>
> *This is why I have often been hindered from coming to you.*

═══ Consider This ═══

Some years back, my friend Nick designed my dream T-shirt. It's a gray T-shirt with simple black lettering and says, "Ask me about my band." I love it so because wearing it creates two opportunities. When someone asks, I can tell them about my country band, J. D. and the Dukes, or I can tell them about my Seedbed band. Or if time permits, I can tell them about both. And in the telling I get them caught up into the fishing net of Jesus.

My band and I tied the first knot on April 8, 2016 (that's 4.8.16 for the numerical mystics among us). At that time I was halfway into the worst and most tragic decade of my life. Two men, about a decade younger than I, approached me with the idea of starting a band. We would invent it as we went—we would build the bridge as we walked across it. We would anchor it in the great tradition of John Wesley and the Moravians before him, and yet we would innovate on the tradition for twenty-first-century application. We knew it was an idea whose time had come again—we desperately needed a deeper form of relationship than the well-meaning but superficial community we had found in our churches.

It turned out that, for the past decade, our friend Kevin Watson had been digging a deep scholarly well into the community structures pioneered by John Wesley. Seedbed published his popular book *The Class Meeting* and subsequently *The Band Meeting*. Kevin famously said the church is addicted to curriculum and it is not adding up to transformational living. We knew he was right and that our own lives were evidence of the deficit.

So on April 8, 2016, Mark and Omar and I started Band #1. I had mentored Omar and Mark about a decade prior through their seminary years when I served as dean of chapel. Little did we know in that first meeting the kind of friendship we would forge together. Almost a decade later, we have met together on most every Friday morning at 8:00 a.m. for our band meeting.

We live in different states, so we meet on a call, connecting in person annually or more as we are able. Here's how the meetings unfold:

After a few minutes of small talk banter, someone will call the band meeting to order with these words:

Wake up, sleepers, and rise from the dead!

And the other two respond:

And Christ will shine on you!

Next, one of us (usually me because I have rememberized it) will pray:

Father, we pray that out of your glorious riches you would strengthen us with power through your Spirit in our inner being. We pray that we would be rooted and established in love so that we, together with all the saints, may have power to grasp how wide and long and high and deep is the love of Christ and that we would know this love that surpasses knowledge that we may be filled to the measure of all the fullness of God. In Jesus's name. Amen.

Next, we take turns responding to five questions:

1. How is it with my soul?
2. What are my struggles and successes?

3. How might God be speaking to me through Scripture and the Spirit?
4. Is there any sin I wish to confess to the band?
5. Is there anything I wish to keep secret from the band?

After one of us finishes responding to the questions (uninterrupted, I might add), the others may speak a word of encouragement and affirmation, and then one of us leads a prayer for the one who shared.

Once all have shared, we conclude the meeting with this prayer:

> *Now to him who is able to do abundantly above and beyond all we can ask or even imagine, according to his power that is at work within us, to him be glory in the church and in Christ Jesus now and throughout all generations. Amen.*

Over the years, we have walked through green pastures, sat by still waters, and helped each other walk through the valley of the shadow of death, disease, divorce, and enormous discouragements. Not only has Jesus preserved our lives through our band, he has transformed us and taught us what real love is—how to receive and give it.

If I may be so bold, I want to make a connection to the work we do with our band to today's text:

> He gave me the priestly duty of proclaiming the gospel of God, so that the Gentiles might become an offering acceptable to God, sanctified by the Holy Spirit.

You see, what we do in relationship with one another is not mere information but transformation. In committing to one another, we become acceptable offerings to God. And I think our world can smell us too.

I'll save the J. D. and the Dukes band story for another study.

The Prayer

Abba Father! Thank you for the gift of each other. You have hidden our inheritance in the saints. Would you give us the courage to begin searching for this treasure in a few other souls? Would you lead us to another two or three people with whom we can become more deeply known and hence more deeply loved? We confess, so often to be well-known is not to be known at all. I want to be known well, and I want to know a few others well. I want to do the work of real soul transformation. I know only you can do that work. I want to learn to show up where that work happens, where I can be transformed instead of endlessly trying to fix myself. Come, Holy Spirit, lead me to this kind of fellowship—for my good, for others' gain, for your glory. In Jesus's name. Amen.

The Questions

Are you ready to launch a band with a couple of people? Are you willing to be made willing? Will you bring this before the Lord as a matter of prayer? What if this is the most significant act of service and mission you could offer your local church or even the church writ large—to tie a knot in the net of the kingdom of God community?

Week 12: Discussion Questions

Hearing the Text

Read Romans 14:13–15:22.

Responding to the Text

- What did you hear?
- What did you see?
- What did you otherwise sense from the Lord?

Sharing Insights and Implications for Discipleship

Drawing from the Scripture text and daily readings, what did you find challenging, encouraging, provocative, comforting, invasive, inspiring, corrective, affirming, guiding, or warning?

Shaping Intentions for Prayer

Write your discipleship intention for the week ahead.

13
WEEK

Romans 15:23–16:27

Romans 15:23–33

85 The Bond of a Band Versus the Rope of Sand

> *But now that there is no more place for me to work in these regions, and since I have been longing for many years to visit you, I plan to do so when I go to Spain. I hope to see you while passing through and to have you assist me on my journey there, after I have enjoyed your company for a while. Now, however, I am on my way to Jerusalem in the service of the Lord's people there. For Macedonia and Achaia were pleased to make a contribution for the poor among the Lord's people in Jerusalem. They were pleased to do it, and indeed they owe it to them. For if the Gentiles have shared in the Jews' spiritual blessings, they owe it to the Jews to share with them their material blessings. So after I have completed this task and have made sure that they have received this contribution, I will go to Spain and visit you on the way. I know that when I come to you, I will come in the full measure of the blessing of Christ.*
>
> *I urge you, brothers and sisters, by our Lord Jesus Christ and by the love of the Spirit, to join me in my struggle by praying to God for me. Pray that I may be kept safe from the unbelievers in Judea and that the contribution I take to Jerusalem may be favorably received by the Lord's people there, so that I may come to you with joy, by God's will, and in your company be refreshed. The God of peace be with you all. Amen.*

Consider This

By the end of Romans 15, we see Paul's fervent commitment to strengthen the church Jesus is building. He has labored through his magisterial letter to mend the net of the little church in Rome. Paul did not see the work of church planting and pastoring as sociological chaplaincy. It was theological and missional. Paul saw these little churches as microcosms of the kingdom of Jesus, little worlds of massive supernatural reality that pointed to the world to come—the new heaven and the new earth. He saw them as communities from that future—for the future—right here in the present. Jesus declared it in his first, seventeen-word sermon:

"The time has come," he said. "The kingdom of God has come near. Repent and believe the good news!" (Mark 1:15)

Jesus wrote the check. Paul was cashing it in every conceivable way. The fishing nets of the kingdom that these little churches represented were being riven by false teaching, stretched out of shape by spiritual warfare, stressed by poverty, and torn by interpersonal conflicts. Paul tied the knots that formed these netlike churches, paid them visits as the Lord allowed, and wrote them letters in between to keep the nets mended and in working order.

Isn't it astonishing how those ancient letters are still mending the nets that are our churches today? As he closes out his letter to the church in Rome, he shares his plan to go to Jerusalem to take an offering for the poverty-stricken church there. After this, he plans to go to Rome, and already he's talking about making Rome the mission base for a fishing expedition to Spain, where he will tie the first knots of a brand-new net (a.k.a. church plant).

You see, Paul knew most deeply that the church is the bond of peace in the unity of the fellowship of the Holy Spirit. It's not an organization set up to provide religious services, spiritual help, and family chaplains. It's not a building to come to and experience good worship and a relevant message. And the church is not "the people"; loosely connected individuals inside a building in Jesus's name merely make up a crowd of Christians. The church rises and falls based on the bonds among us. The connection of deep, bonded attachments among the blood-bought sons and daughters of God, bound together by the Holy Spirit in the very body of Jesus Christ, is the church. In him, we are seated in the house of heaven—and stretching out across the whole earth. It's why our relationships are the mission. It's why awakening rides on the rails of friendship, bound in the knots of our banded fellowship. It's time we started working on the bonds. While there are many ways to do this, I know of none better than the band.

There's a famous conversation from history I reference often in my work. It happened between the celebrated preacher George Whitefield and a man by the name of John Pool, a lesser member of the Methodist movement. Here's the dialogue.

"Well, John, art thou still a Wesleyan?" said Whitefield.

Pool replied, "Yes, sir, and I thank God that I have the privilege of being in connection with him, and one of his preachers."

"John," said Whitefield, "thou art in the right place. My brother Wesley acted wisely—the souls that were awakened under his ministry he joined in class, and thus preserved the fruits of his labor. This I neglected, and my people are a rope of sand."[1]

The Prayer

Abba Father! Awaken us to understand who the church is, whose it is, and what it is in this world. We confess we have organized ourselves in ways that work against what you want to do. Even in coming to our gatherings, we mostly see the backs of each other's heads. We are desperate to see face-to-face and to get to know one another deeply and to learn to love one another profoundly, the way you know and love us. This is what we have to offer the desperate world around us—our very bond with each other in you. Awaken your church. Awaken me. Praying in Jesus's name. Amen.

The Questions

No further questions. Are you ready to do this?

---

1. W. H. Gilder, ed., *The Philadelphia Repository and Religious and Literary Review*, vol. 1 (Philadelphia: Orrin Rogers, 1840), 189.

Romans 16:1–2

86   Phoebe Was a Rock Star

> I commend to you our sister Phoebe, a deacon of the church in Cenchreae. I ask you to receive her in the Lord in a way worthy of his people and to give her any help she may need from you, for she has been the benefactor of many people, including me.

Consider This

Phoebe was a rock star. She was a deacon, which in New Testament terms means she was set apart by Jesus and marked (anointed) by the Holy Spirit in an extraordinary way to do the ordinary work of servant leadership in the kingdom of Jesus. She was a recognized leader in the church in Cenchreae, which in biblical times was the eastern port of the ancient city-state of Corinth. Paul wrote Romans while he was in Corinth.

From all we can tell, Phoebe was a linchpin kind of leader in the early church. You know the type. Paul describes Phoebe as dedicated, hardworking, wealthy, and generous. He called on her to deliver the letter to Rome and most likely to read it for the church, with the same kind of passion, emphasis, and nuance with which Paul would have done himself had he been there.

I love how he referred to Phoebe as "our sister" rather than just "my sister." Here's my question: Why did Paul feel the need to write this?

> I ask you to receive her in the Lord in a way worthy of his people and to give her any help she may need from you.

Could it be because Phoebe was a woman? I'd say probably so. Throughout human history, as a rule, women have been treated as lesser than men, inferior to them, and thereby restricted from full participation in society. Sadly, the church has not only followed suit but often led the way in such treatment.

This is not how it was (or is) in the New Testament church. Of the twenty-six people commended in chapter 16, at least nine of them are women. Jesus's inclusion of women among his disciples was rabbinically revolutionary. Is it any wonder that the women were the last to remain at the cross and the first to arrive at the empty tomb? It was a woman who first proclaimed the resurrection. Mary Magdalene was the apostle to the apostles. Let's not forget our dear sister known to history as "the woman at the well" (a.k.a. Photine), whose witness was so great in the early years of the church that she (along with Mary Magdalene) was given the title "equal to the apostles."[2] It turns out at least seven women were among the twenty-eight witnesses given this designation to date in church history. Among the nine women named in this chapter, he names Junia, a woman regarded as an apostle in the New Testament church.

As we have witnessed in Romans, Paul was writing his letters with the particular purpose to solve specific problems in the little churches. Suffice it to say, when these texts are read in their biblical and first-century context, not to mention the larger biblical narrative, a clear picture emerges that not only supports women in the fulfillment of their various callings to servant leadership across the church but emboldens them.

Phoebe was a rock star.

May her tribe increase.

The Prayer

Abba Father! Thank you that your Son, Jesus, called women into the ranks of his disciples just as he called men. We confess that our own personal history formed by cultural stereotypes and plain, bad teaching has led us to come to the table with a jaded vision. Cleanse us of such prejudices that our vision might be purified to receive and behold revelation in its nuanced depth. You formed us in your image, male and female. Forgive us for the gendered chaos we continue to foment from such simple and divine origins. Awaken us to your creational

---

2. "Samaritan Woman at the Well," Wikipedia, last edited January 31, 2025, https://en.wikipedia.org/wiki/Samaritan_woman_at_the_well.

intentions that we might be fully aligned with the will of your kingdom for the whole world. We pray especially for our daughters today, from infants in our arms through their girlhood and into womanhood. We want them fully invited into and invested in your kingdom to claim their callings and vocations to serve and lead at every level, in every sphere, and in full scope—in the church and as the church in every sector of society. And yes, we pray for our sons to grow up in a divine understanding of manhood as well as a respect for womanhood. All of this for the glory of God in all the world. Praying in Jesus's name. Amen.

The Questions

How does today's teaching resonate with your understanding? Does it challenge you to a deeper and perhaps fuller reading of Scripture? Does it open your eyes to the possibilities we might be missing out on?

Romans 16:3–16

87 | Love Always Has a Name

> Greet Priscilla and Aquila, my co-workers in Christ Jesus. They risked their lives for me. Not only I but all the churches of the Gentiles are grateful to them.
> Greet also the church that meets at their house.
> Greet my dear friend Epenetus, who was the first convert to Christ in the province of Asia.
> Greet Mary, who worked very hard for you.
> Greet Andronicus and Junia, my fellow Jews who have been in prison with me. They are outstanding among[d] the apostles, and they were in Christ before I was.
> Greet Ampliatus, my dear friend in the Lord.
> Greet Urbanus, our co-worker in Christ, and my dear friend Stachys.
> Greet Apelles, whose fidelity to Christ has stood the test.
> Greet those who belong to the household of Aristobulus.

> *Greet Herodion, my fellow Jew.*
> *Greet those in the household of Narcissus who are in the Lord.*
> *Greet Tryphena and Tryphosa, those women who work hard in the Lord.*
> *Greet my dear friend Persis, another woman who has worked very hard in the Lord.*
> *Greet Rufus, chosen in the Lord, and his mother, who has been a mother to me, too.*
> *Greet Asyncritus, Phlegon, Hermes, Patrobas, Hermas and the other brothers and sisters with them.*
> *Greet Philologus, Julia, Nereus and his sister, and Olympas and all the Lord's people who are with them.*
> *Greet one another with a holy kiss.*

Consider This

I'll be honest. For most of my Bible-reading life, I didn't really read chapters like this. I took what I call the Old Testament "genealogy" approach—I skimmed it, which is another way of saying I skipped it. I mean, beyond this text being a marvelous authenticator of the historicity of the ancient document, what's the point of me knowing about people with names like Asyncritus, Phlegm, Philologus, Tryphena, and Tryphosa? (Phlegm? What an unfortunate name!)

Then I saw in my mind's eye the people in the little church I now pastor with names like Tricia, Seth, Laura Beth, Thelma, and Drew. Love always has a name. Asyncritus, Phlegm, Philologus, Tryphena, and Tryphosa—they are now Tricia, Seth, Laura Beth, Thelma, and Drew. From the first century to the twenty-first century, the nets of our local churches come down to the knots and the names, don't they? No names, no knots. No knots, no nets.

Now, because there's a good chance you skipped over the text today, please go back and read it now—and slowly for effect.

Chapter 16 of Romans tells us Paul was good with names, not like a smooth politician but like a person who loved people. Love always has a name. And speaking of names, I've got a bone to pick with many of you—those who regularly say, "I'm not good with names." Have you considered that might mean, "Your name does not matter to me"? In other words, "You really aren't that important to me."

Sure, we all forget names, especially of new people we meet. We don't need more gimmicks to help us remember (though there are worse things). What we need is more love. I'm not particularly good with remembering names either—most of us aren't—but you will never hear those words come out of my mouth. I learned a saying long ago: "A [person's] name is to [them] the sweetest and most important sound in any language."[3]

Imagine how the faces of the people in this Scripture passage lit up as they heard their name read aloud by Phoebe (even Phlegm)! Maybe I'm beyond the scope of the text now, but have you noticed how many people wear name tags these days in our everyday working world? Many workers have their name displayed, from drive-through staff to grocery store workers to call center employees, who always begin by telling you their name. How about we start using their names, with respect and even affection? Did you notice the word that is used seventeen times in today's fourteen verses in this sixteenth chapter? It's *greet*. How about this? Anytime we see someone with a name tag, let's greet them by name. It's one of the little ways of the love of Jesus—making much of other people, celebrating them by speaking their name. What if it's the first sound of awakening to them?

So how about that! The most seemingly irrelevant and formerly skipped-over chapter in the book turns out to hold the most practical implication and application ever!

Love always has a name.

The Prayer

Abba Father! Thank you for knowing us by name, for knowing me by name. Thank you that my name is written in your book. Would you wake me up to this simple act of love, which does require effort, of knowing and greeting people by name, even if that means risking mistakes with new names and

---

3. Dale Carnegie, *How to Win Friends and Influence People* (United Kingdom: World's Work, 1937), 100.

trying again and again until I get it? And let it not be about me but about them. I want to be better at loving people. With the Holy Spirit helping me, I'm going to get good at names. Praying in Jesus's name. Amen.

The Questions

Are you good at remembering and knowing people's names? If not, will you try the name tag experiment, greeting everyone you see today with a name tag and calling them by name? Let me know what happens. And have you ever thought about how much Jesus must love hearing you say his name, especially when you are talking to him?

Romans 16:17–19
88   A Closing Zinger

> I urge you, brothers and sisters, to watch out for those who cause divisions and put obstacles in your way that are contrary to the teaching you have learned. Keep away from them. For such people are not serving our Lord Christ, but their own appetites. By smooth talk and flattery they deceive the minds of naive people. Everyone has heard about your obedience, so I rejoice because of you; but I want you to be wise about what is good, and innocent about what is evil.

Consider This

Just in case you thought it was all rainbows and unicorns from here on out—think again. Paul has a zinger to lodge and a bomb left to drop. It's kind of like unbuckling your seat belt after the plane has landed and you are taxiing to the terminal. Don't do it! Instead, brace for impact.

I appreciate the pull-no-punches nature of the way the Open English Bible translates verses 17–18:

> I beg you, friends, to be on your guard against people who, by

disregarding the teaching which you received, cause divisions and create difficulties; disassociate yourselves from them. For such persons are not serving Christ, our Master, but are slaves to their own appetites; and, by their smooth words and flattery, they deceive simple-minded people. (Romans 16:17–18 OEB)

This is a zinger of a warning against false teaching and false teachers. From the first day to the present day, false teachers and false teaching abound, and they are among the gravest threats to churches then and now.

Please know, this is not Paul warning the church in Rome that the Mormons have moved into the neighborhood. He is talking about church leaders and people influenced by false teaching, errant doctrine, fake gospels, and the like. Notice something else. False teaching, while often cloaked in plausible shifts in interpretive methodology, is usually driven by an attempt to accommodate or otherwise pave the way for the expansion of human appetites and novel ideologies concerning the human body (look up *Gnosticism*). Paul couldn't be any clearer on this point:

> For such people are not serving our Lord Christ, but their own appetites.

Wow, Paul! Jab! Jab! Jab! Here's the right hook:

> By smooth talk and flattery they deceive the minds of naive people.

This is Paul's constant warning to the churches. Remember, he said this in the letter to his protégé Timothy:

> For the time will come when people will not put up with sound doctrine. Instead, to suit their own desires, they will gather around them a great number of teachers to say what their itching ears want to hear. (2 Timothy 4:3)

So what's a Bible-believing, Jesus-following Christian to do? Concerning false teachers and teaching, Paul is emphatic with the Romans: *"Keep away from them,"* says the NIV (emphasis added). The OEB renders it even stronger: *"Disassociate yourselves from them"* (emphasis added).

But why, Paul, what's the harm here? I mean, can't thinking people disagree on such matters? Doesn't it all come down to how you interpret the Bible? Have you looked at the science, Paul? We've heard of your harsh rhetoric concerning women in the church. Why should we be surprised about your other prudish prejudices? (It's a classic tactic of those who can't win on the merits—attack the witness, a.k.a. *ad hominem*.)

But really, why, Paul?

Here's why: False teaching and false doctrine work like termites. They show up long before you have any idea of them, and they slowly, systematically destroy the house from the inside out. By the time you discover their presence, it's usually too late.

Danger, Will Robinson!

The Prayer

Abba Father! Thank you for loving us enough to warn us of the things that will undo us, even when we don't understand, yes even when we disagree. Thank you for the courage of Paul and his tenacity to stand up to the enemies of your church and our souls. Thank you for the thankless love of so many over so many centuries who have stood, at times, against the whole world. Indeed! Praying in Jesus's name. Amen.

The Questions

Do you carry the urgency of Paul's concern about false teachers and false teaching? Or do you have a more laissez-faire attitude?

Romans 16:20-24

89 | Romans 16:19 Says . . .

> *The God of peace will soon crush Satan under your feet.*
>
> *The grace of our Lord Jesus be with you.*
>
> *Timothy, my co-worker, sends his greetings to you, as do Lucius, Jason and Sosipater, my fellow Jews.*
>
> *I, Tertius, who wrote down this letter, greet you in the Lord.*
>
> *Gaius, whose hospitality I and the whole church here enjoy, sends you his greetings.*
>
> *Erastus, who is the city's director of public works, and our brother Quartus send you their greetings.*
>
> - Some manuscripts include here *May the grace of our Lord Jesus Christ be with all of you. Amen.* (v. 24)

Consider This

Lest we forget the biggest of the big picture of the gospel of Jesus Christ, Paul tosses in this closing grenade:

> The God of peace will soon crush Satan under your feet.

There's something beautiful about making this declaration. It's surprising.

After "The God of peace," we might expect something like "will bless you with every blessing in Jesus Christ." Nope.

> The God of peace will soon crush Satan under your feet.

This is straight up *"I believe that we will win!"*

Does Genesis 3:15 ring a bell? It contains the curse of Almighty God against the serpent in the wake of the fall of humankind to his dastardly temptation:

> And I will put enmity
>> between you and the woman,
>> and between your offspring and hers;
> he will crush your head,
>> and you will strike his heel." (Genesis 3:15)

Genesis 3 was clearly echoing in Paul's spirit. Here's the thing about echoes: Their volume diminishes until they can't be heard. This is true with every voice save one: the voice of the Word of God. With God's Word—by the power of the Spirit—the echo gets louder and louder and louder. By the time we get to Romans 16, Jesus has handed Paul the megaphone.

> The God of peace will soon crush Satan under your feet.

There's a little-known Chris Tomlin song I will forever remember. It was one of the songs he wrote before he became Chris Tomlin. ;0) It was back in the late 1900s. Chris, the legendary Bob Swan, and I started a little gathering called "The Harvest" within The Woodlands Methodist Church. On one of those early Sundays, he brought out this song, which he simply called "Romans 16:19." Here are the words.

> Romans 16:19 says
> Romans 16:19 says
> Be excellent in what is good. Be innocent of evil.
> Be excellent in what is good. Be innocent of evil.
> And the God of Peace will soon crush Satan
> God will crush him underneath your feet.
> And the God of Peace will soon crush Satan
> God will crush him underneath your feet.

Repeat twenty times!

I should mention that "Romans 16:19 says" is supposed to be shouted. There is some melody to the lines "Be excellent in what is good. Be innocent of evil." And the last bit that comes from Romans 16:20 is supposed to be declared like a war cry in pure jubilation. In those days, one of our parishioners brought a decibel meter to church each Sunday to subtly hint that the music was too loud! Let's just say I think that was his last Sunday in the Harvest.

Bob Swan, the legendary forty-year youth pastor, pulled together all the youth pastors in the community, and together they launched a Tuesday night weekly meeting. They called it Fresh Vibe. I'll never forget when that massive group met for the first time. Their volume overwhelmed our Harvest crowd, especially when Chris led them in "Romans 16:19." And oh my! That's when it hit me. This is not a war cry. It's a victory lap. It's not a bomb. It's fireworks!

> The God of peace will soon crush Satan under your feet.

The God of peace will soon crush Satan underneath *our* feet because the God of peace has already crushed Satan underneath *his* feet.

The Prayer

Abba Father! Bless you for the gospel, who is Jesus Christ. We love our Savior. The day of march has come now, to make him our Lord—not just a little bit more but completely. We are ready for consecration, utter consecration. We are ready for transformation, complete transformation. We are ready for demonstration, extravagant demonstration. Come, Holy Spirit! Light the fire in our hearts, in my heart. Fan the flames. The God of peace will soon crush Satan underneath our feet. Praying in Jesus's name. Amen.

The Questions

Who's ready to sing "Romans 16:19"? Who's ready to shout it? For you Methodists among us, do you realize you were once called "Shouting Methodists"? Who is ready, in the spirit of King David, to become even more undignified than this? I'll lead the way!

Romans 16:25-27

90 | Now to Him . . .

> Now to him who is able to establish you in accordance with my gospel, the message I proclaim about Jesus Christ, in keeping with the revelation of the mystery hidden for long ages past, but now revealed and made known through the prophetic writings by the command of the eternal God, so that all the Gentiles might come to the obedience that comes from faith—to the only wise God be glory forever through Jesus Christ! Amen.

Consider This

Now we come to the last mile of the marathon that has been Romans. Yes, it's been sixteen chapters, 7,114 words from Paul, and wrapped around that, over sixty thousand words from me. It's like this has been my letters to you concerning Paul's letter to the Romans; meta, huh? Let's be clear, though. Without this magnum opus letter of Paul, there are no letters from me. Apart from the Word of God, I have nothing of consequence to say. Thank God for the Word of God. And all of this is to say, without Jesus, Paul has nothing of consequence to say, no letter to write, no church to encourage, or, as we would say on the farm, "no row to hoe." With three little words, Paul, as they say in gymnastics, "stuck the landing."

> Now to him . . .

Jesus.

All of this is all about Jesus.

Last week, at the time of writing this, I enjoyed one of the single honors of my life. I served as the Bible teacher at Gillett Methodist Church's vacation Bible school. Turns out it was the vacation Bible school for the whole town of six hundred souls. All six churches in Gillett worked together as though they were one church. We had about fifty kids from preschool through fourth grade. My classroom turned out to be the nursery, and we met in a circle of tiny chairs with a little table in the middle. You should have seen me: I had a bag full of props and a bucket full of candy and, yes, a sack full of seeds. They cycled through in age-level groups. The thought struck me more than once during the evening sessions: "Why don't we have vacation Bible school for adults?"

On one of the evenings, we were going over John 3:16. The second graders zealously recited it with me. One of them in particular, Walker, was visibly moved by the verse.

> For God so loved the world that he gave his one and only Son, that whoever believes in him shall not perish but have eternal life.

As the verse ended, Walker raised his hand with an uncontainable urge to speak. As I recognized him, he said to the little circle of his peers and me, "Do you realize God gave his only Son? It was his *only* Son. He didn't have any daughters. He didn't have any other sons. He didn't have twins. It was his *only* Son. Jesus was his only Son, and he came for our salvation."

We all sat there for a minute, stunned, mesmerized by what the second-grader evangelist had said. I'll never forget it.

> Now to Him . . .

> Now to him who is able . . .
> Now to him who is able to establish you . . .
> Now to him who is able to establish you in accordance with my gospel,

That, my friends, is what we want. We want to be established in the gospel of Jesus Christ, the gospel, who is Jesus Christ. This happens as these three words become the go-to words of our everyday lives.

> Now to Him . . .

And those three words become six:

> Now to him who is able . . .

And those six become more words than can be counted. Paul shows us the way. Let's close out with perhaps his greatest "Now to Him":

> Now to him who is able to do immeasurably more than all we ask or imagine, according to his power that is at work within us, to him be glory in the church and in Christ Jesus throughout all generations, for ever and ever! Amen. (Ephesians 3:20–21)

The Prayer

Abba Father! Thank you for Jesus, for your only Son, for loving us so much that you sent him to us. We love you, and now we offer our lives to you. Send us into this world for you, with you, from you, and through you—for them. Now to him who is able. Praying in Jesus's name. Amen.

And let us close with the immortal benediction from the apostle Jude:

> Now unto him that is able to keep you from falling, and to present you faultless before the presence of his glory with exceeding joy, to the only wise God our Saviour, be glory and majesty, dominion and power, both now and ever. Amen. (Jude vv. 24–25 KJV)

The Questions

Now to him who is able . . . How do you fill in the rest of the sentence from your heart, home, church, and city today? Let's go!

Week 13: Discussion Questions

Hearing the Text

Read Romans 15:23–16:27.

Responding to the Text

- What did you hear?
- What did you see?
- What did you otherwise sense from the Lord?

Sharing Insights and Implications for Discipleship

Drawing from the Scripture text and daily readings, what did you find challenging, encouraging, provocative, comforting, invasive, inspiring, corrective, affirming, guiding, or warning?

Shaping Intentions for Prayer

Write your discipleship intention for the week ahead.

Conclusion

Dear saint,

Letters matter.

I know. You're thinking, "Why didn't he begin with, 'Dear Christian'?" Maybe I should close out by saying, "Dear friend." After all, I have written you over ninety letters over these past months together. Truth be told, I wanted to begin that first letter with, "Dear sinner," but I thought you might take that the wrong way. Now you know. Sinner was your original reality. Saint is your new reality. Neither are your identity because your identity is a beloved son or daughter of our heavenly Father. That's the big story of Romans: We are transformed from sinners into saints as we are delivered from slaves into sons and daughters—and all of this by the amazing grace of Jesus Christ.

Letters matter—a lot. Now you can better understand why I claim that Paul's letter to the hundred or so Christians in the ancient city of Rome is the most important letter in the history of the world. Even though that letter wasn't written to us, it was written for us. That's why I have written you these letters—to help make Paul's letter personal for you and me.

I write a lot of letters. Sometimes people write me letters back. I would love it if you would write me a letter. You can send it to my email address: jd@seedbed.com. I'll do my best to write you back.

Here's my bigger challenge: I want to challenge you to become a letter writer. Ask God to show you whom to write to and to help you write them. Just like the Holy Spirit inspired Paul to write to the Romans and just like the Holy Spirit inspired me to write these letters to you, the Holy Spirit will inspire you in your letters. The gold standard of communication in God's kingdom is not a book to the masses but a letter to a person. It can change everything.

Letters matter because letters are seeds. We never know what can come from a single seed. Something tells me you are going to be that kind of sower, because you are already that kind of seed.

I'll see you on the field.

For the awakening,

JOHN DAVID (J. D.) WALT JR.

www.ingramcontent.com/pod-product-compliance
Lightning Source LLC
Chambersburg PA
CBHW011956150426
43200CB00018B/2925